D1558966

PROPHECY SURVIVAL GUIDE
Questions You Ask
copyright © 2000 Book and Video by Russ Doughten Films, Inc.

Published by Russ Doughten Films, Inc. in conjunction with Mustard Seed International, 5907 Meredith Drive, Des Moines, IA. 50322-1204

Except where otherwise indicated, Scripture quotations in this book are from the King James Version

ISBN 1-888568-61-5

Printed in the United States of America.
May 2000

PROPHECY SURVIVAL GUIDE

Featuring Questions You Ask

From the producers of the classic movie series:
A THIEF IN THE NIGHT.

Preface

In March 1998, the Mustard Seed team presented a 'Family Theatre Review' on the first year of their involvement in FamilyNet's Family Theatre television broadcasts. Mustard Seed had entered into the Family Theatre project with some clearly identified criteria, one of which was their insistence on an evangelistic setting for the programs.

FamilyNet, the Southern Baptist Convention's North American Mission Board broadcast arm, was challenging themselves to a higher level of evangelism, and their Program Director, David Lewis, was therefore very enthusiastic about the Family Theatre project, committing time, personnel and resources to the production of the Family Theatre programs.

Using information from the 'Need Him' telephone counseling service, we discovered that hundreds had made a first-time commitment to Christ as a result of that year's transmissions. Encouraged by these results, the Mustard Seed team set themselves the challenge to develop a '5 Star Theatre' television outreach,using the 23 feature films available to them from Russ Doughten Films, Inc.

Once more, David Lewis of FamilyNet cooperated by providing time and resources. The 5 Star Theatre idea became the 'A Thief in the Night Prophecy Mini-Series', five two-hour programs based on the four prophecy films: *A Thief in the Night, A Distant Thunder, Image of the Beast,* and *The Prodigal Planet*, which Russ Doughten Films Inc. and Mustard Seed had been distributing for many years in a variety of formats.

The two hours of programming would need extra material to support the films, and it was decided to create a prophecy question and answer segment for each of the five programs. Dr. Manfred Kober, who had joined the Mustard Seed team, made contact with the leading Bible scholars, Dr. John F. Walvoord, Dr. J. Dwight Pentecost and Dr. J. Randall Price, who willingly cooperated in a two-day film shoot in which they were asked questions and gave brief and to-the-point answers. These answers with Scripture references were inter-cut with selected clips from the four films in the final mini-series programs.

We included brief interviews with members of the cast and crew: Patty Dunning, Don Thompson, Thom Rachford, and Russell S. Doughten, Jr. All contributed their point of view and enriched the program.

The mini-series has since been broadcast many times with numbers of people trusting in Christ as Savior. The 'Questions You Ask' segments have been edited into an eighty-minute video titled 'Prophecy Survival Guide,' released as a companion to this publication. Dialogue from the films and the verbatim text of the answers form the basis of this book.

It was considered appropriate to include many charts and illustrations from Dr. Kober's extensive prophecy library to enrich and support the text.

Finally, we added a number of production stills from the making of the prophecy films as well as brief production notes telling how God guided and provided for the making of the films.

We want to record our thanks to Dr. David Clarke, President, and David Lewis, Program Director, of FamilyNet, for their help and encouragement. Our sincere thanks go to Dr. Bob Record, President, North American Mission Board, SBC, for his support and the excellent gospel appeals he made on the broadcasts.

Our thanks also go to Dr. Walvoord and his staff, and the Dallas Theological Seminary for the use of his office during the filming of the answers segment. A further thank you is extended to Dr. J. Dwight Pentecost and Dr. J. Randall Price for their generous participation.

It is the desire of everyone at Mustard Seed International that this book and the accompanying video may be another evangelistic tool to win many to our Lord Jesus Christ and to instruct believers concerning "things to come."

Layout and Design: Gene McKelvey, Cheryl Neufeld
Project Coordinator, Jimmy Murphy
May 2000

Table of Contents

Introduction

Prophecy Survival Guide: Questions You Ask is a natural outgrowth of the many showings of *A Thief in the Night* and it's sequels around the world. While the films present the answers to many prophecy and salvation issues, they also stimulate the curiosity and imagination of viewers. The answers presented in this authoritative yet easy-to-read collection are a response to these questions.

We want to thank the Bible scholars who enthusiastically contributed time and knowledge to this book. It is their desire that these important prophecies should be clearly understood by their readers. Their individual contribution distinguishes this volume from others.

Our panel of scholars could be a 'who's who' of Bible prophecy knowledge. Their combined teaching, writing and lecturing experience is most impressive. At the end of this book is a list of additional materials from these men. The **Prophecy Survival Guide** scholars are:

Dr. John F. Walvoord (above left), Chancellor and Minister at Large - Dallas Theological Seminary, author.

Dr. J. Dwight Pentecost (right), Distinguished Professor of Bible Exposition, Emeritus - Dallas Theological Seminary, whose book, THINGS TO COME, is recognized as a definitive text book on biblical prophecy.

Dr. Randall Price (left), President of World of the Bible Ministries Inc., conference speaker and Director of World of the Bible Tours.

Dr. Manfred E. Kober (right), Professor of Theology for 30 years at Faith Baptist Bible College in Ankeny, Iowa, Bible Conference speaker, and host of numerous tours to Israel and Europe.

In addition to Bible scholarship, **Prophecy Survival Guide: Questions You Ask** is enriched by the unique insights of people who were involved in the making of the **A Thief in**

the Night film series. The dedication of these talented people has resulted in a film work that has circled the globe and brought the message of salvation to millions.

Russell S. Doughten, Jr. (left), is the Executive Producer of the 'THIEF' end times movie series and plays PASTOR TURNER in the films. Mr. Doughten is President of Mustard Seed International and Russ Doughten Films, Inc.

Donald W. Thompson (right) is the Producer and Director of the 'THIEF' end times movie series and has produced 12 other Christian movies.

Patty Dunning (left) is unforgettable as PATTY, the confused girl pursued by Unite in 'THIEF'.

Thom Rachford (right) created the evil character, JERRY, in the prophecy series and appears in all four of the films. He is the personification of those who sell themselves to the antichrist.

2

A THIEF IN THE NIGHT

RADIO ANNOUNCER: *"...reports keep coming in from all over the globe, confirming it is true. To say that the world is in a state of shock this morning would be to understate the situation. Suddenly and without warning, literally thousands, perhaps millions of people, just disappeared ..."*

FILM CLIP #1 (See the Prophecy Survival Guide video)

A THIEF IN THE NIGHT

What is the rapture?

Dr. Walvoord:

"... the disciples were meeting with Christ for the last Passover. It was actually the fateful night before His crucifixion. Christ told them He was going to leave them and this astounded them and disturbed them because they were expecting Him to bring in His kingdom. And then He tells them He is going to leave them but He is going to the Father's house to prepare a place for them. He doesn't bother to explain because they weren't ready for that. But later when Paul was converted he recorded what God gave him. In 1 Thessalonians 4:13-18 we have a detailed account of how Christ is going to descend from heaven. Christians who have died will be resurrected and living Christians will be raised and instantly changed, and they will be 'caught up' and that's where the word 'rapture' comes from. 1 Thessalonians 4:17, '...be caught up to meet Christ in the air,' and then we'll go from there to heaven. And that is the rapture of the Church.'"

For this we say unto you by the word of the Lord, that we which are alive and remain unto the coming of the Lord shall not prevent them which are asleep.

For the Lord himself shall descend from heaven with a shout, with the voice of the archangel, and with the trump of God: and the dead in Christ shall rise first:Then we which are alive and remain shall be caught up together with them in the clouds to meet the Lord in the air: and so we shall ever be with the Lord.

Wherefore comfort one another with these words.

1 THESS 4:13-18

Dr. Pentecost:

".... the believers in the apostles' day were undergoing intense suffering and persecution: political persecution, religious persecution, economic privation. They had little hope in the surroundings in which they lived. But Paul, writing to Titus,

4

speaks of a 'blessed hope' and that 'hope' is what is referred to as 'the imminent coming of Christ for His own.' By imminent we mean that it is an event that could take place at any moment, at which time blood - bought believers will be translated out of this sphere into the presence of the Father."

Looking for that blessed hope, and the glorious appearing of the great God and our Saviour Jesus Christ.

TIT 2:13

Dr. Price:

"The rapture will happen without warning. Many natural events we prepare for, such as floods, disasters and hurricanes, but with the rapture there is no possibility of preparing, because it has no signs connected with it. The only preparation, the only warning you may receive, is the one you are receiving today. The only preparation you can make is to trust in Jesus Christ as your personal Savior."

In my father's house are many mansions: if it were not so, I would have told you. I go to prepare a place for you.

And if I go and prepare a place for you, I will come again, and receive you unto myself; that where I am, there ye may be also.

JN 14:1-3

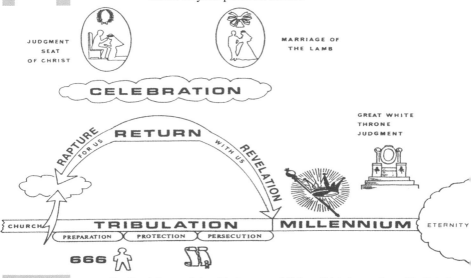

The Church Age concludes with the return of Christ, which is in two phases. The first phase is the rapture of believers, the second phase is the Second Advent of Christ to earth. While believers are in heaven for a time of celebration, the earth will experience a time of unprecedented tribulation. At the Second Advent, Christ establishes His 1,000-year reign on earth. At the conclusion of the millennium, all the unsaved of all the ages will be judged and consigned to the Lake of Fire. Then begins the eternal state.

Dr. Kober:

"The rapture is the first phase of the return of the Lord, followed seven years later by the second phase, which we call the Second Advent or the Revelation of Jesus Christ. At the rapture, Christ comes back for us in the clouds, at the Second Advent, we return with Him to this earth, to rule with Him for 1000 years and all eternity."

Dr. Walvoord:

"If we interpret prophecy literally and pay close attention to the details, the only view that really works is what we call the pre-tribulation rapture, and that means that the rapture is next. It could be today; it could be any moment. It is imminent and it will take out of this world everyone who is born again, who is in Christ, as it states in 1 Thessalonians 4. Nominal Christians will be left behind and others that are unbelievers. So it is very important to be sure that you are a child of God."

Dr. Price:

"1 Thessalonians 1:9 - 10, refers to believers who have trusted God by turning from idols to the true and living God. And they are encouraged to wait for His Son from heaven who delivers us from the wrath to come. It is very important that we recognize that the coming wrath is this great time of tribulation, that the only way out of that is to trust in Jesus Christ, in the Son, and to be waiting for Him, and therefore escape that wrath which is promised to descend on earth."

But as many as received him, to them gave he power to become sons of God, even to them that believe on his name:

JN 1:12

"Men of Galilee" they said, "why stand here looking into the sky? This same Jesus, who has been taken from you into heaven, will come back in the same way you have seen him go into heaven."

Acts 1:11 (NIV)

...in a moment, in the twinkling of an eye, at the last trump: for the trumpet shall sound, and the dead shall be raised incorruptible, and we shall be changed

1 COR 15:52-53

For they themselves show unto us what manner of entering in we had unto you, and how we turned to God from idols to serve the living and true God; and to wait for his Son from heaven, whom he raised from the dead, even Jesus, which delivered us from the wrath to come.

1 THESS 1:9-10

A THIEF IN THE NIGHT

DUANE: " ...*The Bible says, in the twinkling of an eye, millions of people will suddenly disappear, leave this earth to meet their Lord, and a shocked world will discover suddenly that what the Bible said was true...*"

RADIO ANNOUNCER: "...*reports keep coming in from all over the globe, confirming it is true. To say that the world is in a state of shock this morning would be to understate the situation. The event seems to have taken place at the same time all over the world, just about 25 minutes ago. Suddenly and without warning, literally thousands, perhaps millions of people, just disappeared. A few eye witness accounts of these disappearances...*"

FILM CLIPS #2 & 3 (See the Prophecy Survival Guide video)

Will Christians be left behind?

Dr. Kober:

"The rapture includes only believers and yet every believer. The Apostle Paul said in 1 Corinthians 15:51, that every believer will be taken, 'we shall all be changed.' So there are no computer errors. Every genuine believer will be taken into the presence of His Lord."

Behold, I show you a mystery; we shall not all sleep, but we shall all be changed.

1 COR 15:51

The Resurrection of the Dead Saints

The Translation of the Living Saints

A THIEF IN THE NIGHT

DUANE: *"'...so be prepared for you know not what day your Lord is coming.' What does all this mean? It means exactly what it says. Any minute, any second, could be the last chance that anyone has to give himself to Jesus, because when He returns it will happen that fast."*

FILM CLIP #4 (See the Prophecy Survival Guide video)

PRODUCTION NOTES

"We needed the three ferris wheels at the Iowa State Fair set up differently. We asked the owner and he willingly set them up for the movie. He also made the entire area available to us."

Don Thompson, Producer/Director

Do you see signs of the rapture happening soon?

Dr. Walvoord:

"... because the rapture is imminent, by its nature, it can't have signs, because it is going to come at any time. But there is a question, because 2000 years have elapsed since Christ made that prediction. How soon will the rapture occur? And the fact is that the Bible doesn't give us a specific answer. But it does describe in great detail the events that will follow the rapture: the great tribulation and the things that precede that, and the changes in Israel, the nations and the Church, all of which are going to take place at the end times. And also the revival of the Roman Empire will occur. Now all of these things are in a movement stage. The last 50 years have seen tremendous changes, all of which seem to point to the conclusion that the stage is all set for the rapture and the events that will follow . . .and the rapture could be very soon."

And ye shall hear of wars and rumors of wars: see that ye be not troubled: for all these things must come to pass, but the end is not yet.

For nation shall rise up against nation, and kingdom against kingdom: and there shall be famine, and pestilence, and earthquakes, in diverse places.

All these are the beginning of sorrows. Then shall they deliver you up to be afflicted, and shall kill you: and ye shall be hated of all nations for my name's sake.

And then shall many be offended, and shall betray one another, and shall hate one another.

And many false prophets shall rise, and shall deceive many. And because iniquity shall abound, the love of many shall wax cold.

MATT 24:6-12

O YE HYPOCRITES, YE CAN DISCERN THE FACE OF THE SKY: BUT CAN YE NOT DISCERN THE SIGNS OF THE TIMES?

MT 16:3

RUSSIA

ISRAEL

UNITED NATIONS

ECUMENICAL MOVEMENT

In the tribulation, Israel will be back in the land. Also, a one-world government and one-world apostate church will emerge. And, at the mid-point of the tribulation, Russia (Gog and Magog, Ez. 38-39) will attack Israel.

Today, we are observing the emergence of these movements which will find their culmination after the rapture. It is of great prophetic significance that we are witnessing a one-world government in the UNO, that Israel is an independent nation, that Russia is flexing her military muscles, and that the ecumenical movement is in the process of forming a one-world church.

Dr. Pentecost:

"The rapture is a signless, timeless event. That meant that believers in every day had the same 'Blessed Hope' that they could be translated out of the earthly sphere, caught up into the presence of our Lord. The events that are given in Scripture to herald the approach of the Second Advent were God's gracious opportunity given to unbelievers to turn in faith to Jesus Christ, for at His Second Advent Jesus Christ is coming as Judge. And to meet Him in judgment means to be consigned to an eternity apart from Christ. Therefore God gives them an opportunity by signs preceding the advent to turn in faith to Him."

Dr. Kober:

"There are no signs for the rapture, actually, but signs that relate to the period following the rapture, the tribulation. Israel will be back in the land, there will be a one-world apostate church and a one-world government. Present developments in these areas are signs pointing ahead to the tribulation period."

Immediately after the tribulation of those days shall the sun be darkened, and the moon shall not give her light, and the stars shall fall from heaven, and the powers of the heavens shall be shaken: And then shall appear the sign of the Son of man coming in the clouds of heaven with power and great glory.

MATT 24:29-30

But yourselves know perfectly that the day of the Lord so cometh as a thief in the night.

2 THESS 5:2

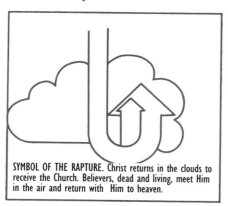

SYMBOL OF THE RAPTURE. Christ returns in the clouds to receive the Church. Believers, dead and living, meet Him in the air and return with Him to heaven.

A THIEF IN THE NIGHT

PATTY in telephone booth: *"I don't know, yeah, the dam?"*

"How am I going to get to the dam?"

"Okay Jerry. Okay, I'll get there. Just wait!"

FILM CLIP #9 (See the Prophecy Survival Guide video)

Will anyone be saved during the tribulation?

Dr. Pentecost:

"Revelation 7 makes it clear that multitudes from every kindred, tongue, tribe and nation will wash their robes and make them white in the blood of the Lamb during the seven years of the tribulation period. The gospel will be proclaimed by God's chosen witnesses and they will blanket the earth with the message of salvation through Jesus Christ. Some wonder how this can happen, for they misunderstand Paul's teaching in 2 Thessalonians 2, supposing that the Holy Spirit will be removed and therefore no one can be saved. However, the Holy Spirit is not indwelling the Body, the Church, as His Temple during that period but He is omnipresent and no one in any age has ever been saved apart from the work of the Holy Spirit. He will be active to an a l m o s t unprecedented degree during the years of the t r i b u l a t i o n period."

And say unto them, Thus saith the Lord God; Behold. I will take the children of Israel from among the heathen, whither they be gone, and will gather them on every side, and bring them into their own land:

EZEK 37:21

And now ye know what withholdeth that he might be revealed in his time.
For the mystery of iniquity doth already work: only he who now letteth will let, until he be taken out of the way.

2 THESS 2:6-7

144,000 witnesses are sent out into all the earth. REV 7:1-7, 14:1-5

Dr. Walvoord:

"The way of salvation is the same in all ages. It is all based on the death of Christ, His shed blood and our faith in Him. And while in the Old Testament they only partially understood it, they had to trust God. And in the tribulation time it is going to be the same way. They are saved by trusting in Christ. The dilemma is of course that there is going to be such opposition of Satan and such satanic deception that it's going to be difficult for them to do it!"

Dr. Pentecost:

"Salvation is offered today as God's free gift through His grace, based on the blood of Christ. It costs one little today to receive such a gracious gift. During the tribulation period, those who accept Christ will face martyrdom at the hands of the Beast because of their faith."

And he[Abraham] believed in the Lord; and he counted it to him for righteousness.

GEN 15:6

After this I beheld, and, lo, a great multitude, which no man could number, of all nations, and kindreds, and people, and tongues, stood before the throne, and before the Lamb, clothed with white robes, and palms in their hands.... And I said unto him, Sir, thou knowest. And he said to me, These are they which came out of great tribulation, and have washed their robes, and made them white in the blood of the Lamb.

REV 7: 9,14

For by grace are ye saved through faith; and that not of yourselves: it is the gift of God: Not of works, lest any man should boast.

EPH 2:8-9

PATTY DUNNING

Narrator:

"Patty was one of the leading characters of these films. She now lives in Des Moines, Iowa, with her husband and two daughters. We asked Patty how she felt about making these films and what impact it had on her life."

Patty Dunning:

"As I look back, my feelings now are just, just being amazed that God even allowed me to be a part of the work that was done and has been done since that time. And I am really humbled knowing what an imperfect person I am, and just being able to be a part of His message to people and how it affected so many people, including myself, my family, friends, for so many years now. So I hope to get to do it again!"

A THIEF IN THE NIGHT

PASTOR BELVEDERE: *"There will be no place to hide."*

FILM CLIP #6 (See the Prophecy Survival Guide video)

Narrator:
"Patty were you ever afraid?"

Patty Dunning:
"Oh, at different times it wasn't very hard to be fearful. Like when I'd have to go down through a field, with what I thought were just millions of bugs, you know, that kind of thing, or when I was lying under that pendulum and realizing, if that thing fell down, I would be in big trouble. I think the hardest thing was, in part, imagining that this was the end of the world, or it could be, and realizing that I would be without family and I would be without the God that people had been telling me about but that I didn't know. So I think that was a little bit harder but as a new believer I was able to do it."

How powerful is the antichrist?

Dr. Walvoord:

"The antichrist is, of course, the one who is going to rule the world in the period after the rapture until the Second Coming. He is going to be controlled by Satan. And we are told that he has power from Satan. Revelation 13 is an amazing revelation of this. It first of all describes that he suffers an assassination attempt. At least I interpret it that way. I don't believe antichrist will be killed. Satan can't restore life to the dead but he can heal. And this man comes on the scene as a supernatural person. And the whole world, according to Revelation 13, is going to worship him. But the power behind him is Satan, instigating all of his opposition to Christ and his opposition to the saints of God."

And I saw one of his heads as if it were wounded to death;and his deadly wound was healed: and all the world wondered after the beast.

And they worshiped the dragon which gave power unto the beast:and they worshiped the beast, saying, Who is like unto the beast? Who is able to make war with him?

REV 13:3-4

Dr. Pentecost:

"In the Revelation 13 there are three different spheres in which antichrist will operate by Satan's power. In verse 7 he has power in the political realm, so that he becomes head of a one - world govern-

A THIEF IN THE NIGHT

TELEVISION ANNOUNCER: *"...report today to your local UNITE Identification Center and show yourself to be a true citizen of the world."*

FILM CLIP #7 (See the Prophecy Survival Guide video)

PRODUCTION STILL

Location setup in the downtown area of Des Moines.

ment. In verses 17 and 18 he becomes the head of a one - world economy and he so controls that no man can buy or sell unless he has that mark. And then in verse 8 he is head of a one - world religion in which he becomes the object of worship. All of his power is derived from Satan. According to verse 2 Satan gives him his power and his throne and great authority."

Dr. Price:

"During the tribulation period, we are told that the antichrist causes all, small and great, to receive a mark and this mark, it says, is the number of his name, which means that these people are identified with his program and with his person. All those who take the mark will be able to buy and sell and trade in that day. Those who do not will be put to death. There is a false prophet who causes all, both small and great, to worship the antichrist and take his mark. Now today many people realize that there are a lot of religions and they are confused about what to believe. In that day, however, the deception will be so great that it is imperative that in this hour, while there is still the clear message of the truth, people understand and trust in Jesus Christ who is the coming Savior!"

antichrist and false prophet, who are the and second beasts of Revelation 13.

And the beast which I saw was like unto a leopard, and his feet were as the feet of a bear, and his mouth as the mouth of a lion: and the dragon gave him his power, and his seat, and great authority....

And it was given unto him to make war with the saints, and to over-power them: and power was given him over all kindreds, and tongues, and nations....

And he causeth all, both small and great, rich and poor, free and bond, to receive a mark in their right hand, or in their foreheads: And that no man might buy or sell, save he had the mark, or the name of the beast, or the number of his name.

REV 13:2,7,16-17

And they overcame him by the blood of the Lamb, and by the word of their testimony; and they loved not their lives unto death.

Therefore rejoice, ye heavens, and ye that dwell in them. Woe to the inhabitants of the earth and of the sea! For the devil is come down unto you, having great wrath, because he knoweth he hath but a short time.

And when the dragon saw that he was cast unto the earth, he perse-cuted the woman which brought forth the man child.

REV 12:11-13

A THIEF IN THE NIGHT

REVEREND TURNER: *"...how many, how many have I misled? How many are still here because of me? It was all there. I read it. I studied it. I preached it, it really didn't matter. How many are still here because of me?"*

FILM CLIP #8 (See the Prophecy Survival Guide video)

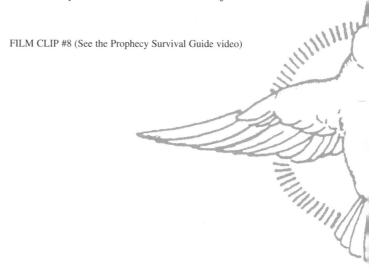

What happens to the Holy Spirit?

Dr. Kober:

"The Holy Spirit will still be here. It is just that some of His Church age activities will be gone, such as the baptizing work of the Holy Spirit, the universal permanent indwelling, as well as the restraint of sin."

Dr. Price:

"According to 2 Thessalonians 2, there is a restrainer that is taken out of the way. Many interpret that to be the Holy Spirit working through the Church, who restrains evil in society in general. If that is the case, then the Holy Spirit is removed with the Church. However, His presence universally has not been removed. It remains on the earth with a different function."

And now ye know what withholdeth that he might be revealed in his time.

For the mystery of iniquity doth already work: only he who now letteth will let, until he be taken out of the way.

2 THESS 2:6-7

A THIEF IN THE NIGHT

JAIL MATRON: *"...and they said you don't want to be identified! I suspect there is a misunderstanding."*

PATTY: *"I know what is going on and it's evil. It may be too late for me, and I'm not going to join it!"*

JAIL MATRON: *"Does this look like a 666 to you?"*

PATTY: *"Look, I'm not stupid. I know that's a computer read-out for 666."*

FILM CLIP #9 (See the Prophecy Survival Guide video)

PRODUCTION NOTES

Don could not find a location for A Distant Thunder. One day in Sears, Don noticed a kitchen setup that looked exactly like the one he had used for A Thief in the Night. Sears' people agreed to allow him to use it, assuring us tremendous savings in not having to build the set!

What will people's attitudes be?

Dr. Pentecost:

"In Revelation 13, we are introduced to the ministry of a false prophet who, by Satan's power, performs a multitude of miracles to convince the world that antichrist is actually God. The deception will be so successful that multitudes will offer worship to this satanic deceiver."

Dr. Walvoord:

"The world as a whole is going to be deceived by the false prophet and will believe that the antichrist is God on the basis of the miracles that he has performed. But that, of course, is a fulfillment of prophecy 'that they believe not... they will believe the lie.'"

Dr. Price:

"Even today people say that they will believe anything as long as it is not written in the Bible. In the tribulation period they will find that the Bible has predicted all the events that will come and the reality is that at that time, the book will be quite clear.....and therefore the trust that people should have in it and obeying its message is paramount."

...and deceiveth them that dwell on earth by the means of those miracles which he had power to do in the sight of the beast; saying to them that dwell on the earth, that they should make an image to the beast, which had the wound by a sword, and did live.

REV 13:14

And for this cause God shall send them strong delusion, that they should believe a lie:

2 THESS 2:11

A DISTANT THUNDER

WOMAN: *"...you have got to help me! I can't take the mark! ...My baby is dying..."*

CLINIC EMPLOYEE: *"Look! I don't make the rules, I only obey them. If you want your child cared for, you must have your ID. Otherwise, go!"*

FILM CLIP #10 (See the Prophecy Survival Guide video)

What about children in the rapture?

Dr. Kober:

"This is one of those areas in the Bible where God is silent. However, I personally believe that God does not divide families. If parents are taken up in the rapture, probably these children who have not yet had an opportunity to believe in Christ will also be taken with their parents rather than be left behind."

Shall not the Judge of all the earth do right?

GEN 18:25

Dr. Price:

"I think we can leave this in the hands of a sovereign God but we have an implication in 1 Corinthians 7: 14, where it talks about a home where there is an unbelieving spouse present. It says there that the believing spouse sanctifies that relationship so that these children are holy. In that case, it seems that children will go in the rapture with the believing spouse. But there is also the possibility that children will be left with unbelievers in the rapture as well."

Infants are covered by the blood of Christ. MATT 19:13-14, (...."of such is the kingdom of Heaven.")

A DISTANT THUNDER

PATTY inside church: *"Come on, do you expect me to love a God who has caused all these hideous things to happen? If God really loved me, then why am I having to go through all these things?"*

KENT: *"Patty, these days of tribulation are God's way of letting evil destroy itself. If you turn your back on God now you'll be destroyed!"*

FILM CLIP #11 (See the Prophecy Survival Guide video)

Why does God let bad things happen?

Dr.. Walvoord:

"People are unsaved and they have departed from the grace of God and there is no forgiveness apart from the grace of God. And the result is that they have asked God, in effect, to stay out of their lives and the result is that terrible things do overcome them. And God is just allowing the natural results of sin to take place."

Dr. Pentecost:

"God is a God of grace and a God of love and He desires to bring men to Himself, to the salvation that He has provided. Throughout Scripture it is evident that God has sought to get the attention of men by subjecting them to discipline. The tribulation period is a time of judgment in which God is seeking to bring people - through those judgments - to the end of themselves, and to bring them to faith in Jesus Christ, so that they might enter into the blessings that the Son of God will provide for His believers at His Second Advent."

And he shall confirm the covenant with many for one week: and in the midst of the week he shall cause the sacrifice and the oblation to cease, and for the overspreading of abominations he shall make it desolate, even until the consummation, and that determined shall be poured upon the desolate.

DAN 9:27

Thus he said, The fourth beast shall be the fourth kingdom upon the earth, which shall be diverse from all kingdoms, and shall devour the whole earth, and shall tread it down, and break it in pieces.

And the ten horns out of this kingdom are the ten kings that shall arise: and another shall rise after them; and he shall be diverse from the first, and he shall subdue three kings.

And he shall speak great words against the most High, and shall wear out the saints of the most High, and think to change times and laws: and they shall be given into his hand until a time and times and the dividing of time.

DAN 7:23-25

A DISTANT THUNDER

PATTY inside shop: *"...that's what I hate about religion. God makes all these elaborate plans to send us to hell!"*

JENNY: *"Patty, God made a perfect plan that none should perish. He sacrificed His Son to keep you from hell."*

PATTY: *"Well, I'm glad it works for you, Jenny. I don't know... what's that?"*

JENNY: *"This is a tribulation map."*

FILM CLIP #12 (See the Prophecy Survival Guide video)

When does the tribulation start?

Dr. Kober:

"Many people believe that the tribulation begins immediately after the rapture. I think there is a short preparatory period. We don't know how long that period will be. But during that period to which Christ refers in Matthew 24:8 as 'the beginning of sorrows,' there will be many false christs and many false prophets. One of these false christs will emerge as the political leader on the scene, and the tribulation proper begins when the antichrist makes a covenant of peace with Israel. According to Daniel 9:27, that covenant is broken in the middle of the tribulation period, but the tribulation begins with this covenant."

Dr. Walvoord:

"'The tribulation' is often used to refer to the entire period between the rapture and the Second Coming - a period longer than seven years. I can briefly survey this. First of all there's the revival of the Roman Empire. The antichrist takes control of first three countries - then all ten. Then he makes a seven - year covenant of peace

And he shall confirm the covenant with many for one week: and in the midst of the week he shall cause the sacrifice to cease, and for the overspreading of abominations he shall make it desolate, even until the consummation, and that determined shall be poured upon the desolate.

DAN 9:27

Thus he said, The fourth beast shall be the fourth kingdom upon the earth, which shall be diverse from all kingdoms, and shall devour the whole earth, and tread it down, and tread it in pieces.

And the ten horns out of this kingdom are ten kings that shall arise: and another shall arise out of them; and he shall be diverse from the first, and he shall subdue three kings.

And he shall speak great words against the most High, and shall wear out the saints of the most High,

continued

On location during the filming of A Distant Thunder.

with the Middle East and Israel. And for 3 1/2 years there is relative peace, though there is some trouble and an invasion from the north. But then, in the last 3 1/2 years, is what Christ in the book of Revelation calls, 'the great tribulation.' And that's the 3 1/2 year period that Christ refers to as so awful that if He didn't stop it there would not be any human beings left. So, while the word 'tribulation' refers to the whole period, 'the great tribulation' refers to the last 3 1/2 years."

and think to change times and laws: and they shall be given into his hand until a time and times and the dividing of time.

DAN 7:23-25

For then shall be great tribulation, such as was not since the beginning of the world to this time, no, nor ever shall be.

And except those days should be shortened, there should no flesh be saved: but for the elects sake those days shall be shortened.

MATT 24:21-22

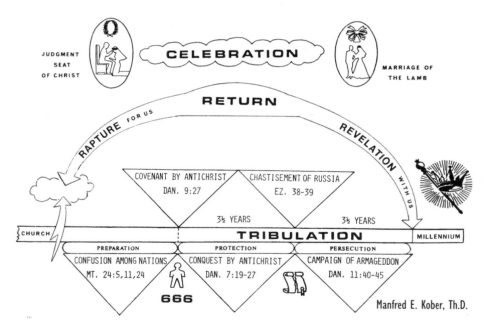

Manfred E. Kober, Th.D.

Between the rapture and the Second Advent, five major geo-political events will occur on earth. Immediately after the rapture, numerous false christs and false prophets will emerge. At the beginning of the tribulation the antichrist makes a covenant with Israel, then gains control over a ten-nation confederacy. After Russia invades Israel and is totally destroyed; the antichrist extends his reign of terror world-wide. He and the armies of the world are embroiled in a bloody carnage at Armageddon as Christ returns with the saints from heaven to supplant the impostor and begin His millennial reign.

A DISTANT THUNDER

SANDY in living room: *"...Look at this: July 16th. Almost two months ago Brother Christopher signed a pact with Israel and the ten nations."*

WENDA: *"What does that mean?"*

SANDY: *"Well, remember Patty, when the evangelist told us that when that happened it was the beginning of the seven-year tribulation."*

PATTY: *"...that's right!"*

DIANE: *"...Hey, come on girls, this isn't the end of the world!"*

PATTY: *"...Maybe not, but I have a feeling that we're going to wish it was."*

FILM CLIP #13 (See the Prophecy Survival Guide video)

What will happen to those who believe?

Dr. Kober:

"There are three possibilities concerning those who trust in Christ in the tribulation period. Some will be executed by antichrist - Revelation 20:4. Others will escape to a mountain refuge east of the Dead Sea, which Christ mentions in Matthew 24:16. And yet others will somehow perish from the exposure to the various judgments of the tribulation period."

And I saw thrones, and they sat upon them, and judgment was given unto them: and I saw the souls of them that were beheaded for the witness of Jesus, and for the word of God, and which had not worshiped the beast, neither his image, neither had received his mark upon their foreheads, or in their hands; and they lived and reigned with Christ a thousand years

REV 20:4

JEWS FROM JERUSALEM ESCAPE TO AMMON, MOAB, AND EDOM IN THE MIDDLE OF THE TRIBULA-TION.
MT 24:15-22,
REV 12:13-16,
IS 63:1-4
DAN 11:41

A DISTANT THUNDER

GUARD in church: *"Our great Brother Christopher is so concerned with your welfare and your future, that he has provided a way for you to avoid going to your death. All you have to do is to get up from where you're seated and come forward to receive your ID. It's painless, much like the credit cards you've used for many, many years."*

GRANDMA in kitchen: *"...the only people who won't want the mark are those who become believers and a lot of those will be killed by the beast or antichrist."*

PATTY: *"You mean a person can become a Christian after the rapture?"*

GRANDMA: *"The 144,000 sealed missionaries from Israel will be responsible for leading multitudes to receive Christ as their Messiah."*

FILM CLIP #15 (See the Prophecy Survival Guide video)

Dr. Walvoord:

"In Revelation 7 we are given two tremendous revelations. First of all, there will be 144,000 Israelites - 12,000 of each tribe - that are preserved, in the sense that they are physically kept from being killed during the great tribulation. In chapter 14, at the end of the tribulation, they are still existing. And that, of course, proves that God can protect His people."

Dr. Pentecost:

"According to Revelation 7, the 144,000 are physical descendants of Abraham, who are sovereignly set apart by God to fulfill the ministry that God purposed for the nation of Israel, when He chose them as His people. They were to be God's lights to the world. Israel failed to fulfill that. But during the tribulation period these 144,000 will fulfill the function that God intended for Israel, and will become God's light to the Gentiles."

And I saw another angel ascending from the east, having the seal of the living God: and he cried with a loud voice to the four angels, to whom it was given to hurt the earth and the sea, saying, hurt not the earth, neither the sea, nor the trees, till we have sealed the servants of God in their foreheads.

And I heard the number of them which were sealed: and there were sealed an hundred and forty thousand of all the tribes of the children of Israel.

REV 7:2-4

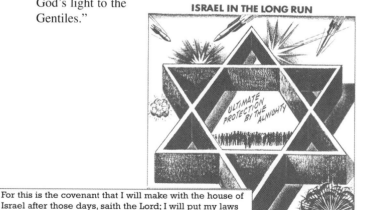

ISRAEL IN THE LONG RUN

ULTIMATE PROTECTION BY THE ALMIGHTY

For this is the covenant that I will make with the house of Israel after those days, saith the Lord; I will put my laws into their mind, and write them in their hearts: and I will be to them a God, and they shall be to me a people.

___HEBREWS 8:10

A DISTANT THUNDER

MISSIONARY: *"For God so loved the world, that he gave his only begotten Son, that whosoever believeth in him should not perish, but have everlasting life."*

WENDA: *"I do believe, what must I do to be born again?"*

MISSIONARY: *"Admit you're a sinner, that Christ shed His blood and died for your sins, that He was resurrected and is truly the living Son of God."*

FILM CLIP #16 (See the Prophecy Survival Guide video)

Are the judgments literal?

Dr. Price:

"The book of Revelation records both justice on the unrighteous as well as rewards for the righteous. If we get rid of one - making the judgments symbolic - then the other, the rewards, must also be symbolic. No one wants to get rid of the eternal promises of heaven. At the same time, when Jesus was on the Mount of Olives, He warned - literally - His disciples to flee the coming wrath, to flee Judea, to flee to the mountains. And therefore He was not warning them to flee from symbols but from the literal judgments that are coming."

We have also a more sure word of prophecy; whereunto ye do well that ye take heed, as unto a light that shineth in a dark place, until the day dawn, and the day star arise in your hearts: Knowing this first, that no prophecy of the scripture is of any private interpretation.

For the prophecy came not in old time by the will of man: but holy men of God spake as they were moved by the Holy Ghost.

2 PET 1:19-21

Dr. Kober:

"I believe the Bible should be interpreted literally, in its normal, customary sense, and that includes prophetic portions as well. At the time of its writing, one fourth of the Bible was predictive prophecy. Half of it has been fulfilled - and fulfilled in a literal way, so that we may well infer that

A THIEF IN THE NIGHT

TV ANNOUNCER: *"Religious leaders have stated that today's events were foretold in the Bible thousands of years ago. One religious leader quoted Revelation 6:4 'And there went out another horse that was red and the power was given to him that sat thereon to take peace from the earth and that they should kill one another. And there was given unto him a great sword.' Again the Bible haunts us with passages that used to sit on dusty shelves, now becoming screaming headlines!"*

FILM CLIP #17 (See the Prophecy Survival Guide video)

the unfulfilled portion of the Scriptures will also be fulfilled literally. For instance, in Revelation 6 we read of a horseman who will bring about the death of one-fourth of the world's population. And that judgment, as well as the other judgments, we need to take very literally and seriously."

"God, the architect of the ages, has seen fit to take us into His confidence concerning His plan for the future and has revealed His purpose and program in detail in the Word. A greater body of Scripture is given to prophecy than any other one subject, for approximately one-fourth of the Bible was prophetic at the time it was written. That portion was devoted to the unfolding of God's program. Because of its prominence in Scripture it is only natural that much should have been written on the subject."

J. Dwight Pentecost, *Things to Come*, Preface, vii

PRODUCTION NOTES

We needed a cave scene. God led us to Ruidoso, New Mexico, and a cave near Fort Wingate. It was a nationally protected bat cave. We were told that as long as we were out before the bats returned in October, we could use it. It proved to be the perfect site.

Don Thompson, Producer/Director

A THIEF IN THE NIGHT

PATTY: *"Why didn't you tell us all this before it was too late?"*

REVEREND TURNER: *"Patty, do you have a Bible?"*

PATTY: *"Well, yes!"*

REVEREND TURNER: *"What does it say?"*

PATTY: *"What?"*

REVEREND TURNER: *"Does it say that Christ died for your sins? Does it say that if you ask for forgiveness and receive him into your heart, that you will be saved?"*

PATTY: *"Yes!"*

REVEREND TURNER: *"Then, why are you blaming me?"*

PATTY: *"Because you could have preached it. You never even talked about prophecy and you criticized the evangelist for using scare tactics. I would rather have been scared into heaven than have to go through this!"*

REVEREND TURNER: *"You could have received Christ the night the evangelist was here!"*

What about today's storms and earthquakes?

Dr. Pentecost:

"In Revelation 4, God is being honored as the Creator. As the Creator, He is sovereign over all nature. Storms, hurricanes, tornadoes are all under His control. They always have been. They will be under His control during the tribulation period. But because there seem to be unprecedented storms today, does not mean those are the storms of the 7 years of the tribulation period. God will demonstrate that all creation is subject to the authority of the Creator, and the storms will try to attract their attention to bring the creature in subjection to the Creator, so that they might be saved from the wrath to come."

...the twenty and four elders fall down before him that sat on the throne, and worship him that liveth for ever and ever, and cast their crowns before the throne, saying, thou art worthy, O Lord, to receive glory and honour and power: for thou hast created all things, and for thy pleasure they were and are created.

REV 4:10-11

A DISTANT THUNDER

GUARDS: *"Remove your blindfold. ...I understand you are having a hard time making a decision."*

PATTY: *"How would you know that?"*

WENDA: *"You know, the medic at the hospital seemed to know an awful lot about us also."*

GUARD: *"Some of your friends are kind of concerned about your future. I think you ought to hear what they have to say."*

WENDA AND PATTY: *"Jenny! Jenny! You're a Christian!"*

JENNY: *"Oh, Patty, anybody can say they're a Christian!"*

FILM CLIP #19 (See the Prophecy Survival Guide video)

Will believers be persecuted?

Dr. Walvoord:

"In the great tribulation, first of all, they will try to require everyone to worship and obey the antichrist, and the penalty for not doing this is death. There is evidence that there will be thousands of people taken to the guillotine - martyrs to their faith - who will refuse to denounce Christ and accept the antichrist as their God. There, of course, will also be the mark of the beast which is necessary to buy or sell. You can't buy food for your family or sell anything or do anything. You can't get medicine. All of the normal things of life will be disrupted. In other words, you are enduring terrible persecution and you may lose your life in the process."

Dr. Kober:

"Christ speaks of these persecutions in Matthew 24:9, 'They shall deliver you up to be afflicted, and shall kill you, and you shall be hated of all nations for my name's sake.'"

And when he had opened the fifth seal, I saw under the altar the souls of them that were slain for the word of God, and for the testimony which they held: And they cried with a loud voice, saying, How long, O Lord, holy and true, dost thou not judge and avenge our blood on them that dwell on the earth?

REV 6:9-10

Are these films based on true stories?

Don Thompson:

"These motion picture stories are all fiction, of course, but the prophecy is not. I have always believed that if the audience doesn't believe your story, they're not going to believe your message. In these pictures we've created characters so that - Patty Dunning for example - the audience identified with her because she was not a believer. So when she got into situations where she got into trouble, the audience began to root for her. And at the end of the picture, when she still hadn't given her life to Christ, the audience wanted her to and so with an open end - we left it open for you to receive Christ into your heart."

THIEF IN THE NIGHT

DONALD W. THOMPSON

Narrator:

"The Thief in the Night mini-series was written and directed by Don Thompson. We asked Don, 'What was the purpose of these films?'"

Don Thompson:

"Once I received Jesus Christ into my heart, my life changed so drastically and so wonderfully that I wanted everybody to have what I had. I wasn't a preacher. I wasn't a writer. I didn't know how to present this message of who Jesus Christ was, but the way that I tell it was on film. I wanted everybody to know who Christ is and to receive Him, because He's coming back soon and if people don't know Him, they are going to spend eternity in hell without Christ."

A DISTANT THUNDER

WOMAN in hospital: *"My baby is dying!"*

HOSPITAL LADY: *"Look! I don't make the rules, I only obey them! If you want your child cared for you must have your ID. Otherwise, go!"*

. . .

PATTY in church: *"Its so ironic, that night the evangelist was at our church, he asked people to come forward to receive Christ. It would have been so simple then! And now we have to go forward and reject Christ or be killed! Oh, if we had only done it then, only done it then."*

EVANGELIST: *"God loves you and wants to save you, but it's up to you!"*

FILM CLIP #20 (See the Prophecy Survival Guide video)

Will medical help be refused?

Dr. Pentecost:

"The satanic deceiver seeks to imitate and claim for himself all of the prerogatives that belong to almighty God. In order to demonstrate that he is absolute sovereign, he will refuse any help, food, clothing, shelter, medicine to those who don't submit to him and receive the mark of the beast."

For false Christs and false prophets shall rise, and shall show signs and wonders, to seduce, if it were possible, even the elect.

MK 13:22

Dr. Price:

"The tribulation will be a terrible time in which judgment is poured out on the world. The antichrist will ravage the earth and all who are on it. But today, God in His goodness and His grace and His love, extends the opportunity to all who will to come to Him and believe His good message, that whoever believes in the Lord Jesus Christ shall be saved. So now is the hour - now is the time to come to Jesus Christ - personally."

HEB. 3:7, 8
To-day if ye will hear his voice,
Harden not your hearts; as in the provocation, in the day of temptation in the wilderness:

A DISTANT THUNDER

REVEREND TURNER: *"The sting is terrible. It doesn't kill you; it just leaves you in a state of torment for five months. Only those sealed by God will be exempt. It's an intense, horrible torment. Death will be preferable, but not possible. Trumpet number six consists of two hundred million horses and horsemen loosed to destroy one third of the earth's population."*

PATTY: *"Two hundred million horses?"*

PATTY: *"There were that many horses in China in the late seventies, Cathy! Anyway, the seventh trumpet is a review of all the others. It is a warning to men. Cathy, this is not God's temper tantrum. It's a sifting process to get the lost to respond to Christ."*

FILM CLIP #21 (See the Prophecy Survival Guide video)

What is the purpose of Bible prophecy?

Dr. Walvoord:

"Prophecy was indicated to us to give us events that are going to happen in the future, in order that we may prepare for them now. And that's especially important in the matter of salvation, because we need to trust in Christ now, and be born again by trusting in the Lord who died for us and rose again, and who has promised salvation to all who come to Him in faith. And if we do that now, then we'll be raptured and won't enter into the troubled tribulation that those who do not have Christ will experience, because they're going to be left behind."

Then shall they deliver you up to be afflicted, and shall kill you: and ye shall be hated of all nations for my name's sake And many false prophets shall rise, and shall deceive many.

MATT 24:9-11

Dr. Pentecost:

"Every reference to the coming of Christ in the New Testament epistles is followed by an exhortation to godliness, to holiness, to righteousness in daily living. That is why although it is called the 'blessed hope' and a 'comforting hope,' it is referred to by John as 'the purifying hope.' It was to transform our daily conduct in the light of the coming of the One for Whom we are waiting."

THE RAPTURE IS

1. A BLESSED HOPE
"looking for that blessed hope and the glorious appearing..."   Titus 2:13

2. A PURIFYING HOPE
"And every man that hath this hope in him purifieth himself, even as he is pure."   1 John 3:3

3. A COMFORTING HOPE
"Wherefore comfort one another with these words."
                                      1 Thessalonians 4:18

4. A SURE HOPE
"We have also a more sure word of prophecy; whereto you do well that you take heed."   2 Peter 1:19

PRODUCTION STILL

PRODUCTION NOTES

The filming at the railroad bridge was in serious trouble. A highway patrolman stopped and asked, "Are you having trouble?" "Yes," said Don, "we need to park our trucks on the shoulder of the interstate!" God again watched out for us. Three Highway Patrol cars directed the busy interstate for the rest of the day while the helicopter menaced Patty on the bridge.

For the Christian, the Bible provides clear and detailed teachings concerning the future, so that we may know with certainty what lies ahead... the knowledge of prophecy provides joy in the midst of affliction, cleanses and encourages holy living, is profitable, like all Scripture, for a number of important needs in the Christian's life, gives facts about life after death, gives truth about the end of history, gives proof of the reliability of all Scripture, for the number of prophecies that have come to pass precisely as predicted cannot be accounted for by chance but only by God. And finally, prophecy draws our hearts out in worship to the God who is in complete control and who will accomplish His will in history. To slight prophecy is to miss these benefits.

Adapted from Charles C. Ryrie, *Basic Theology,* 439-440

And the Spirit and the bride say, Come. And let him that heareth say, Come. And let him that is athirst come. And whosoever will, let him take the water of life freely. REV. 22:17

IMAGE OF THE BEAST

WORLD CHURCH SPEAKER: *"How can the corporations cooperating with the church profit from the defeat of Israel? One of our greatest assets is, of course, that Brother Christopher, as President of the Federated States of Europe, has been elected to lead us, giving us a vision and a sense of leadership second to none."*

FILM CLIP #22 (See the Prophecy Survival Guide video)

PRODUCTION NOTES

While shooting in Des Moines near a park, we discovered that cross-country races were being held in the same area. We set up and rehearsed the stunt drivers' moves and wondered what would happen. When no runners were visible, Don cried, "Action," and the shot was taken just before the next runner appeared. All day, as if on cue, a runner would appear just after the shot was done.

Don Thompson, Producer/Director

Will there be a church during the tribulation?

Dr. Kober:

"At the rapture, of course, every true believer will be gone, but religious people will still be left behind, and these will join into a one-world church - or the ecumenical church - probably comprised of apostate Protestantism, Roman Catholicism, and the world's non-Christian religions. Revelation 17 speaks of that system as the scarlet woman riding the scarlet beast."

Dr. Walvoord:

"The word 'church' applies to this particular work of God that began on the day of Pentecost, and apparently concludes with the rapture. And so the word 'church' doesn't appear in Revelation 4 and following - once we get past the seven churches of Asia. And I take it that there is no real church there until she reappears as the wife of Christ, just before the millennial kingdom."

So he carried me away in the spirit into the wilderness: and I saw a woman sit upon a scarlet coloured beast, full of names of blasphemy, having seven heads and ten horns.

And the woman was arrayed in purple and scarlet colour, and decked with gold and precious stones and pearls, having a gold cup in her hand full of abominations and filthiness of her fornication.

REV 17:3-4

Symbol of the World Council of Churches which spearheads the ecumenical movement

IMAGE OF THE BEAST

UNITE AGENT: *"Release him!"*

JERRY: *"Who?"*

UNITE AGENT: *"You know who!"*

JERRY: *"What?"*

UNITE AGENT: *"Listen the cashier at Food Center 33 said that the woman indicated that she was going to see the High Priest next month."*

JERRY: *"Which means?"*

UNITE AGENT: *"If the woman does attend the event she may be the bait to lure the fish! Release David Michaels, give him a pair of boots, plant a transmitter and tail him. If the plan works, we've got them both."*

JERRY: *"David, you are an amazing fellow, a very talented individual. You have a list of charges against you that would normally cause the authorities to take your head with a golden blade. Murder, fraud, resisting the authorities, trying to infiltrate our security system - hey - not to mention the fool you made out of me!"*

Dr. Price:

"The tribulation will be a very religious age. People will not be able to deny the things that take place on earth: all the judgments are coming from heaven at the same time the antichrist will be receiving world-wide worship. There will be an apostate church that gives them that kind of acknowledgment. It's important for us to remember that today there are many religious people - sincere and socially respectable - that may not have a personal relationship with Jesus Christ. In order to avoid becoming a part of that kind of apostate church, it is important to have a personal faith in Jesus Christ."

The Scarlet Woman of Revelation 17. (Illustration from Luther's December Testament, 1522)

IMAGE OF THE BEAST

REVEREND TURNER: *"Then a great leader will rise up and save Israel. He will appear to be slain, then Satan will enter into him and counterfeit his resurrection. This great leader will then pronounce himself world dictator, destroy the world church and be proclaimed greater than God. He will seize the Temple, set up his image and begin the most devastating persecution in the history of Israel."*

DAVID: *"Doesn't Satan understand prophecy?"*

REVEREND TURNER: *"Perhaps not fully, but according to James 2:19 he knows God's Word and he believes it!"*

FILM CLIP #24 (See the Prophecy Survival Guide video)

Will Satan be involved?

Dr. Pentecost

"The principal characters in the tribulation period, such as the beast and the false prophet, receive their power from Satan, so that Satan is the one in absolute authority over all of the events that transpire through the beast and the false prophet. They are instruments to glorify Satan - to bring honor to him that belongs to God alone."

Dr. Walvoord:

"Satan will be empowered with a supernatural power that manifests itself in the tribulation with the idea of causing people to worship the antichrist as God. He performs miracles as the Scriptures testify and Revelation 13 clearly indicates. But the fact is that the second half of the last seven years will be especially satanic, because the Scriptures record in chapter 12 that he is thrown out of heaven, where previously he has been allowed to accuse the brethren of sinning. And the Scriptures record that he knows that his time is short. He believes in the Second Coming and he is doing all he can to bring trouble to the world. That's why it is 'the great tribulation,' that Christ says is so awful, that if it were not for His coming to stop it, that no creature would be left alive."

...and there was war in heaven: Michael and his angels fought against the dragon; and the dragon fought and his angels, and prevailed not; neither was their place found any more in heaven.

And the dragon was cast out, that old serpent, called the Devil, and Satan, which deceiveth the whole world: he was cast out into the earth, and his angels were cast out with him.

And I heard a loud voice saying in heaven, Now is come salvation, and strength, and the kingdom of our God, and the power of his Christ: for the accuser of our brethren is cast down, which accused them before our God day and night.

And they overcame him by the blood of the Lamb, and by the word of their testimony; and they loved not their lives unto the death.

REV 12:7-11

IMAGE OF THE BEAST

GUARD in prison cell: *"You're next!"*

MISSIONARY at guillotine: *"Jesus said in John 14:6, 'I am the way, the truth and the life and no man cometh to the Father but by me.'"*

"John revealed so beautifully that 'God so loved the world, that he gave his only begotten Son, that whosoever believes in him shall not perish, but have everlasting life!' Oh, how God loves us, how God loves us!"

FILM CLIP #25 (See the Prophecy Survival Guide video)

Will there be a counterfeit trinity?

Dr. Kober:

"Satan has always been the great counterfeiter. Ever since his fall when he said 'I will be like God,' rather than 'I will be unlike God' in Isaiah 14, he has tried to counterfeit the plan and program of God. This is especially true in the tribulation period when he has his christ on the throne. Many Bible students have noticed that in the tribulation period there is indeed the unholy trinity, comprised, of course, of Satan himself who is the anti-father, of the antichrist - who is the second person of the unholy trinity, and the false prophet - the anti-spirit. So, indeed, we have an unholy trinity for seven years on this earth."

SATAN
ANTI-FATHER

THE UNHOLY TRINITY
REV 13

MAN OF SIN
ANTICHRIST

FALSE PROPHET
ANTI-SPIRIT

Dr. Price:

"In Revelation 13 we have three individuals mentioned. Two are called beasts - one is referred to as antichrist, and the other one is the false prophet, and the third is called the dragon. And that is Satan, clearly the head of this counterfeit trinity. Then there is the antichrist who takes the place, in the sense of Christ, and the false prophet who speaks in his name - like the Holy Spirit. So there seems to be this kind of deceptive allure in the last days to draw people to the false apostate church and its religion."

And I stood upon the sand of the sea, and saw a beast rise up out of the sea, having seven heads and ten horns, and upon his horns ten crowns, and upon his heads the name of blasphemy.

And they worshiped the dragon which gave power unto the beast: and they worshiped the beast, saying, Who is like unto the beast? Who is able to make war with him?

And I beheld another beast coming up out of the earth; and he had two horns like a lamb, and he spake as a dragon.

REV 13:1,4,11

THE PRODIGAL PLANET

VOICE at missile launch: *"Permission to fire? Missile away!"*

NARRATOR: *"With a noise like that of chariots they leap over the mountain tops like a crackling fire consuming stubble, like a mighty army drawn up for battle. At the sight of them nations are in anguish, every place turns pale. But Jesus said in John 3:16, 'For God so loved the world, that he gave his only begotten son, that whosoever believes in him shall not perish but have eternal life.'"*

FILM CLIP #26 (See the Prophecy Survival Guide video)

For God sent not his Son into the world to condemn the world; but that the world through him might be saved. JN. 3:17

What will life be like for unbelievers?

Dr. Walvoord:

"There's going to be a terrible time of trouble for everybody. Those who are not saved will have pressure to worship the beast and receive his mark, which will assure their ultimate condemnation. And those who will not, are faced with the prospect of being executed for their lack of obedience to the world ruler. And it's going to be a terrible time of trouble, all of which could have been avoided, if they had accepted Christ before the rapture of the church and would have been raptured when Christ came."

Dr. Pentecost:

"The wrath of God is awesome, and the prophets describe it as a day of darkness, of gloominess, of unprecedented fear and terror falling upon men."

And he causeth all, both small and great, rich and poor, free and bond, to receive a mark in their right hand, or in their foreheads: And that no man might buy or sell, save he that had the mark, or the name of the beast, or the number of his name.

REV 13:16-17

THE PRODIGAL PLANET

DAVID: *"Where are we going?"*

CONNIE: *"Away from that! We are about five and a half miles from what appears to be ground zero. We were lucky, David! All we got was the tail end of that fire storm but when the radiation hits the ground we don't want to be under it."*

DAVID: *"It seems hard to believe that God could use something that hideous for good! But He's done it before!"*

FILM CLIP #27 (See the Prophecy Survival Guide video)

Will there be nuclear explosions?

Dr. Walvoord:

"It could be that there are some nuclear explosions, but the Bible itself seems to attribute these things to God. In other words, nuclear weapons couldn't make the sun reduce its light - or the moon. And it couldn't cause missiles to fly from heaven. It couldn't cause earthquakes. In other words, these are things that God inflicts upon the scene, and I'm inclined to think that most of the terrible things that happen are judgments of God - the expressions of His wrath on a world that has rejected Christ and is attempting to accept an impostor - a man who is actually Satan - dominated."

And I will show wonders in the heavens and in the earth, blood, and fire, and pillars of smoke. The sun shall be turned into darkness, and the moon into blood, before the great and terrible day of the Lord come.

And it shall come to pass, that whosoever shall call on the name of the Lord shall be delivered: for in mount Zion and in Jerusalem shall be deliverance as the Lord hath said, and in the remnant whom the Lord shall call.

JOEL 2:30-32

Not only **SAVED**, (Gal. 1:4)
but **SAFE**. (John. 10:28)

THE REDEEMED OF THE LORD

"In the hollow of His hand."

THE PRODIGAL PLANET

DAVID: *"Hey! You look great, you look great! I'm really glad to see you, Matthew!"*

REVEREND TURNER: *"Well my goat's gone and so are my chickens! But I got fresh meat and a place to sleep. You're welcome to stay."*

DAVID: *"Stay where? What happened to your barn?"*

REVEREND TURNER: *"Well lightening struck it some time ago. I took everything I could salvage and moved underground. Actually, it's the first time anyone has dropped in since I moved!"*

FILM CLIP #28 (See the Prophecy Survival Guide video)

Are the bowl judgments the worst?

Dr. Price:

"The bowl judgments come as the last of a sequence of judgments, beginning with the seal judgments, the trumpet judgments, and finally the bowl judgments. And the picture is that of a great bowl - which is the wrath of God - and the angels turn it upside down, pouring it out, so that every single drop of the wrath of God is exhausted on earth. And so the bowl judgments are the most severe, ending with hundred - pound hailstones plummeting to the earth and bringing great destruction."

Dr. Walvoord:

"They are the climax of the wrath of God which has continued ever since the beginning of the great tribulation, particularly, and of course prepare the way for the Second Coming of Christ. It's obvious that they extend to the whole earth, in contrast to the trumpet judgments that only went to a third, in some cases. And it also deals with a great earthquake that's going to remove mountains. And islands are going to disappear. The whole earth configuration is going to be changed, with the possible exception of the land of Israel. And this, of course, is something that

And the seventh angel poured out his vial into the air; and there came a great voice out of the temple of heaven, from the throne saying, it is done.

And there were voices, and thunders, and lightnings; and there was a great earthquake, such as was not since men were upon the earth, so mighty an earthquake, and so great. And the great city was divided into three parts, and the cities of the nations fell: and great Babylon came in remembrance before God, to give unto her the cup of the wine of the fierceness of his wrath.

And every island fled away, and the mountains were not found.

REV 16:17-20

The Sixth Seal Judgment of Revelation 6:12-15. (Illustration from Luther's New Testament of 1524)

the world has never seen before and will never see again. It's a terrible, terrible climactic judgment from God."

Dr. Pentecost:

"Throughout Scripture when God disciplines the people, He begins gently and increases the severity of the disciplines, until the discipline has accomplished His purpose. That seems to be true in the progression through the seals, and the trumpets, and the bowl judgments - each increases in intensity until the wrath of God comes to its climax in the bowl judgments, associated with the Second Advent of Christ back to the earth."

And there fell upon men a great hail out of heaven, every stone about the weight of a talent: and men blasphemed God because of the plague of the hail; for the plague thereof was exceedingly great.

REV 16:21

For as the lightning cometh out of the east, and shineth even unto the west; so shall also the coming of the Son of man be.

MATT 24:27

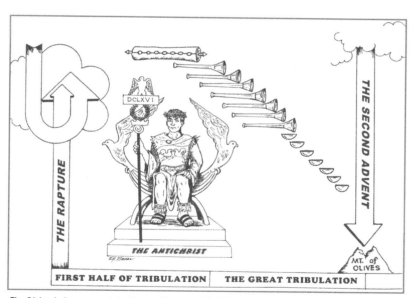

The Divine Judgments and the Human Dictator of the Tribulation.   Manfred E. Kober, Th.D.

THE PRODIGAL PLANET

DAVID: *"Connie, what are you thinking?"*

CONNIE: *"Ah, I was thinking about Turner. Strange! I mean, he seems to know a lot about the Bible and yet he doesn't seem to be a believer. And, apparently, he doesn't want to be one!"*

DAVID: *"The idea of salvation seems to torment him."*

CONNIE: *"But he has all that knowledge!"*

DAVID: *"I wonder if maybe he isn't being eaten alive by all that knowledge and the guilt of not having preached God's word to his congregation. He seems to have a compulsion to learn all he can in order to work out his own plan for salvation."*

• • •

DAVID: *"Open up the door. We don't want to hurt you. We'll take you. Come on, open up!"*

LINDA: *"Who are you?"*

DAVID: *"Look, no mark!"*

FILM CLIP #29 (See the Prophecy Survival Guide video)

Will people get saved in the tribulation?

Dr. Price:

"Throughout all the ages, from the beginning to the end, salvation is by grace through faith in Jesus Christ. It will be no different in the tribulation period. However, the conditions will be far more severe, and coming to faith in Christ will be a far more difficult thing - it will cost one's own life, many times, in order to make that important decision. How important it is while we have the convenience and the unimpeded opportunity, at the present time, to put our trust in Christ and escape the coming wrath!"

And I saw another angel fly in the midst of heaven, having the everlasting gospel to preach unto them that dwell on the earth, and to every nation, and kindred, and tongue, and people,

REV 14:6

Dr. Kober:

"I believe that in the coming tribulation an unprecedented number of people will be saved. We are told in Revelations 7 that for the entire seven year period of time, 144,000 witnesses will minister to the people on earth. Imagine what it's going to be like with 144,000 Apostle Paul's turned loose! There will be two witnesses ministering. According to Matthew 17:11, Elijah will come again. And then toward the end of the tribulation period an angel will preach the gospel in every nation (Revelation 14:6). We are told twice that people - large, innumerable multitudes - will be saved, from every place on this planet, even from countries where people have heard the gospel in the church age."

Location filming for Image of the Beast.

PRODUCTION NOTES

Heidi Vaughn flew to Des Moines for one scene. A doll wrapped like a baby was ready but just as we were going to shoot, a young mother volunteered to allow her baby to be in the scene. Would the baby react appropriately? When Heidi became hysterical the baby began to cry and we got the pictures. Once more God met our needs in a way we never expected.

Don Thompson, Producer/Director

SALVATION IN THE TRIBULATION

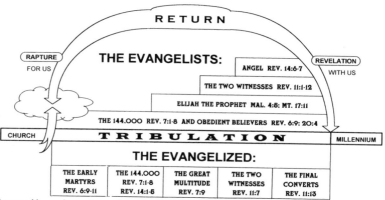

RETURN

RAPTURE — FOR US

THE EVANGELISTS:

ANGEL REV. 14:6-7

REVELATION — WITH US

THE TWO WITNESSES REV. 11:1-12

ELIJAH THE PROPHET MAL. 4:5; MT. 17:11

THE 144.000 REV. 7:1-8 AND OBEDIENT BELIEVERS REV. 6:9; 20:4

CHURCH

T R I B U L A T I O N

MILLENNIUM

THE EVANGELIZED:

THE EARLY MARTYRS REV. 6:9-11	THE 144.000 REV. 7:1-8	THE GREAT MULTITUDE REV. 7:9	THE TWO WITNESSES REV. 11:7	THE FINAL CONVERTS REV. 11:13

The preaching and acceptance of the gospel during the tribulation.　　　Manfred E. Kober, Th.D.

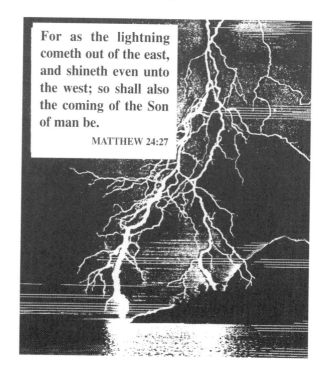

For as the lightning cometh out of the east, and shineth even unto the west; so shall also the coming of the Son of man be.

MATTHEW 24:27

THE PRODIGAL PLANET

DAVID: *"Does it seem real now?"*

LINDA: *"All I know is that God took my dream and turned it into something ugly! I'll tell you what's real David: thirst, hunger, heartbreak and fear!"*

DAVID: *"Did you ever think that maybe it wasn't God that shattered your dream. Maybe it was sin that shattered your dream? It did mine and others like us. Because we chose to live our lives our way instead of God's!"*

FILM CLIP #30 (See the Prophecy Survival Guide video)

What are the trumpets and the seals?

Dr. Price:

"The seal judgments are the inaugural judgments that begin the tribulation, with the four horsemen of the Apocalypse, bringing cold war on the earth. They, with the trumpet judgments and the bowl judgments that follow, are sequential and progressive and they esca-

late as we go through the tribulation. The seal judgments begin to unleash all kinds of famine and war on earth and are clearly judgments. But the wrath of God has much more to do. When we come to the trumpet judgments, we find almost the exact duplicate of the plagues that were poured out on Egypt during the Exodus, including all the different kinds of pestilence. And they escalate and they cause people to cry out and cause them to repent and turn to the God of Heaven."

And I saw in the right hand of him that sat on the throne a book written within and on the backside, sealed with seven seals.
And I saw a strong angel proclaiming with a loud voice, Who is worthy to open the book, and to loose the seals thereof?

REV 5:1-2

For centuries artists have attempted to illustrate end-times prophecy. This illustration portrays the Seven Trumpet Judgments of Revelation chapters 8 and 11 (from Luther's Complete Bible of 1534).

PRODUCTION NOTES

A huge barn was built in Indianola, Iowa. A living room was constructed on twenty-one telephone poles so that we could shake it for the earthquake scene. Over forty various moves had to be made during the 'quake.' Rehearsal began at 8 a.m. for this 'one take' shot and the film had to be approved by the lab before we could burn down the barn.

Don Thompson, Producer/Director

Dr. Kober:

"Some Bible scholars believe that these judgments are similar or repetitive. I think there is a chronological sequence from the seven seal judgments to the seven trumpet judgments to the seven bowl judgments. In Revelation 6 we read of the seven seals. The last of the seals issues into the seven trumpet judgments. And then the seventh trumpet judgment issues into the seven bowl judgments. These judgments increase in rapidity, severity, and intensity as the tribulation period moves along."

THE SEAL JUDGMENTS
1 White Horse & Cold War
2 Red Horse & Open War
3 Black Horse & Famine
4 Pale Horse & Death
5 Martyrs in Heaven
6 Physical Disturbances
7 Rev. 8:1-6

THE TRUMPET JUDGMENTS
1 Catastrophes on Earth
2 Convulsions on Seas
3 Pollution of Waters
4 Darkening of Heavens
5 Torment of Humans
6 Death of 1/3 of Mankind
7 Rev. 11:15-19

THE BOWL JUDGMENTS
1 Sores upon Mankind
2 Death in the Sea
3 Rivers Turned to Blood
4 Scorching of Mankind
5 Darkness and Pain
6 Euphrates Dries Up
7 Earthquake, Hail & Death
(Rev. 16)

THE PRODIGAL PLANET

CONNIE: *"David, I've got a signal, its strong."*

BROTHER CHRISTOPHER: *"...and I say, let us break their bonds asunder and cast their cords from us. I am the Prince of this world. In my name and in the power of my glory with advanced missile and nuclear technology, we will blow this self-righteous God from His throne. You can see via satellite we are already moving equipment towards Palestine. Soon He will not plague us anymore with famine and fire, with pittance and pestilence. We will meet this God of tears and torment in the valley of decision. We will settle once and for all who will be king!"*

FILM CLIP #31 (See the Prophecy Survival Guide video)

How powerful is the antichrist?

Dr. Walvoord:

"The power of the antichrist is obviously absolute and he has all power, but he's still hindered by God. God can control him and keep him down. And it's still true that even if this man of sin desires to do something, he doesn't necessarily bring it about all over the earth."

Surely the wrath of man shall praise thee: the remainder of wrath shalt thou restrain.

PS 76:10

Dr. Kober:

"It seems as though Satan gives his personal power to the antichrist, because according to Revelation 13, antichrist is in control of the world's nations. He is economically in control. No one can buy or sell unless he has the mark of the beast on his hand or his forehead. And he will have total religious authority, because all those who refuse to bow down and worship him will be beheaded."

Satan empowers and manipulates antichrist and the false prophet.

THE PRODIGAL PLANET

JODI: *"What happens to the people who get a dose of radiation that's not fatal?"*

LINDA: *"Well, it depends on the amount they receive,. but in most cases the radiation destroys the white blood cells which means they have no immunity."*

JODI: *"Is that what the doomsday people suffer from?"*

LINDA: *"Uh huh, and even if they catch a common cold it'll kill them."*

JODI: *"What happens if they just get a little bit?"*

LINDA: *"Oh, the symptoms vary, but they could get boils."*

• • •

RICK: *"Boils? Carbuncles! The stupid things are driving me nuts."*

FILM CLIP #32 (See the Prophecy Survival Guide video)

Will evil dominate?

Dr. Kober:

"I definitely think that evil will dominate the world, because, for one thing, the restraining ministry of the Holy Spirit will be gone. And then too, Satan will give his personal evil power to the antichrist, according to 2Thessalonians 2:9 and Revelation 13:2. And antichrist will be in total dominion over this wicked world system, empowered by Satan until such a time that Jesus Christ returns and supplants antichrist."

Even him, whose coming is after the coming of Satan with all power and signs and lying wonders ...

2 THESS 2:9

Dr. Pentecost:

"Satan is working his plan and purpose to dethrone God and to enthrone himself, through the beast and the false prophet, as his principal agents in the tribulation period. Since he is 'the' evil one, his evil will be perpetrated in the earth to an unprecedented degree. So it will be a period of unprecedented sin, darkness, and lawlessness here on the earth."

And the beast which I saw was like unto a leopard, and his feet were of a bear, and his mouth as the mouth of a lion: and the dragon gave him his power, and his seat, and great authority.

REV 13:2

How has your life been touched by being in these films?

THOM RACHFORD

Narrator:

"Jerry took the mark and served the antichrist in these films. His real name is Thom Rachford, from Los Angeles. Thom, what was the impact of these films in your life?"

Thom Rachford:

"Well, I feel blessed. I always wanted to be an actor and God gave me that opportunity with these films. But even more than the opportunity to be an actor was to do something that was significant for the kingdom. There is no greater blessing than knowing that you have been a part of a special work that the Lord has provided and given you the opportunity to be a part of it. My favorite part is when people come up to me and say, something like, 'Excuse me, this is going to sound funny, but are you in a movie?' I like it when people do that. That is a blessing."

"The impact on my life - working on these films - first of all, was to give me a greater understanding of God's plan for mankind and what I believe is the near future of the world. But on a personal basis, it has made me more desirous to share who Jesus is with people and to perfect my personal witness. And I try to do that not only on a personal level, but I also have greatly inspired to do that with my church and also through the 'Share Your Faith' Seminars which help equip Christians to better share who Jesus is and what a new life with Him can be. That impact has caused a deeper relationship for me, with Jesus."

THIEF IN THE NIGHT

THE PRODIGAL PLANET

JODI: *"Before you start talking to me about God, you'd better prove to me that there is one, 'cause he certainly hasn't shown me much....How far is it across this stupid land until we get to where we are going?"*

DAVID: *"You in a hurry?"*

JODI: *"I'm bored!"*

DAVID: *"You're not the least bit concerned about what I said out there, are you?"*

JODI: *"Should I be?"*

DAVID: *"Anything could happen to you. Today, tomorrow, you could have a blood clot hit your brain and drop dead as we talk!"*

JODI: *"You think I care? Anything is better than this!"*

DAVID: *"Even hell?"*

FILM CLIP #33 (See the Prophecy Survival Guide video)

Will people believe the lie?

Dr. Price:

"2 Thessalonians 2:11 says that all those who rejected Jesus Christ before the rapture will after the rapture believe a lie. This lie, according to 2 Thessalonians 2:4, is the antichrist's deception that he is deity. He will usurp the place of God, exalt himself above every so called god and object of worship and seat himself in the Jewish Temple in Jerusalem. He will be accompanied by the false prophet, with all false wonders and signs and the world will be persuaded by a great delusion that this is so!"

Dr. Walvoord:

"The lie is that Jesus Christ is not God and that the antichrist is. And this is the test that has been mentioned, demonstrated by miracles and all these things, as he claims to be God and sits in the Temple accepting worship. And those who believe the lie will, of course, be lost and con-

Let no man deceive you by any means: for that day shall not come, except there come a falling away first, and that man of sin be revealed, the son of perdition;

Who opposeth and exalteth himself above all that is called God, or that is worshiped; so that he as God sitteth in the temple of God, shewing himself that he is God.

2 THESS 2:3-4

A THIEF IN THE NIGHT

VOICE #1 at missile launch: *"94 automatic firing. Prepare to fire a missile. Prepare to fire. Indicator blue.*

VOICE #2: *"Permission to fire?"*

"Missile away!"

NARRATOR: *"But Jesus said in John 3:16, 'For God so loved the world, that he gave his only begotten Son, that whosoever believes in him shall not perish but have eternal life.'"*

FILM CLIP #34 (See the Prophecy Survival Guide video)

PRODUCTION NOTES

The cobra used in the film was provided by the Des Moines Children's Zoo. It refused to come out of the cage but the handler pulled it out and we filmed it pulling itself back inside. We reversed the footage and you see it coming out.

Don Thompson, Producer/Director

demned when Christ comes back in the Second Coming."

Dr. Pentecost:

"When Jesus Christ was here on earth the first time, He introduced Himself as the Son of God, and this claim was authenticated by the multitude of miracles that Jesus performed. When antichrist appears, he will claim to be God. And the false prophet will authenticate antichrist as God, the same way that Jesus Christ was authenticated as the Son of God, by miracles and signs."

And then shall that Wicked be revealed, whom the Lord shall consume with the spirit of his mouth, and shall destroy with the brightness of his coming:

Even him whose coming is after the working of Satan with all power, and signs, and lying wonders,

2 THESS 2:8-9

And the third angel followed them, saying with a loud voice, if any man worship the beast and his image, and receive his mark in his forehead, or in his hand,

The same shall drink of the wine of the wrath of God, which is poured out without mixture in the cup of his indignation; and he shall be tormented with fire and brimstone in the presence of the holy angels, and in the presence of the Lamb:

REV 14:9-11

Antichrist and the false prophet desecrate the temple. (MT 24:15, 2 THESS 2:4)

THE PRODIGAL PLANET

CONNIE: *"You wait till I'm half dead before you show up! Your choppers always bring my fuel, my rations late! Why did you put me through all this?"*

HERB: *"We have had a few problems of our own lately, young lady! Our equipment got so hot we couldn't use it. Aircraft blew up in hangars! If you hadn't let them run off without you in Omaha this wouldn't have happened!"*

CONNIE: *"I told them to go. My training officer failed to tell me when these would appear!*

HERB: *"So everybody's got 'em!"*

CONNIE: *"Believers don't get them!"*

FILM CLIP #35 (See the Prophecy Survival Guide video)

What about the two witnesses?

Dr. Walvoord:

"The two witnesses in Revelation are witnesses to the power of God in the midst of unbelief in the world, and there is some question as to whether it's the first half or the second half of that last seven year period. I think it is the second half. And they witness throughout the great tribulation. And then God permits their enemies to kill them and their bodies lie in the streets of Jerusalem for 3 1/2 days and then suddenly God raises them from the dead. They ascend into heaven. And there is an earthquake in Jerusalem that destroys one tenth of the city. And so we have the fact that these two witnesses are the true witnesses of God. The Bible does not give us their names, and while some have tried to name them, I prefer to leave them unnamed."

And after three days and a half the Spirit of life from God entered into them, and they stood on their feet; and great fear fell upon them which saw them.

And they heard a great voice from heaven saying unto them, Come up hither. And they ascended up to heaven in a cloud; and their enemies beheld them.

And the same hour was there a great earthquake, and the tenth of the city fell, and in the earthquake were slain of men seven thousand: and the remnant were affrighted, and gave glory to the God of heaven.

REV 11:11-13

Dr. Pentecost:

"The two witnesses, according to Revelation 11, are prophets. Prophets

God loved and gave — Man believes and lives

GOD'S SIDE — MAN'S SIDE

"For God so loved the world, that He gave His only begotten Son, that whosoever believeth in Him should not perish, but have everlasting life."

John 3:16

THE BIBLE IN A NUT-SHELL

PRODUCTION NOTES

Stan and Jean Whipple of Indianola moved out of their farm for a month, allowing us to use the interior and the exterior. We also built a barn on their property and burned it down. Jean often got up at 3 a.m. and baked peach pies for the entire cast and crew.

Don Thompson, Producer/Director

were God's messengers to bring God's message
to the nation Israel. They appear in the same city
were Jesus Christ was crucified, that is,
Jerusalem. Jesus had said that the gospel of the
kingdom would be preached and these two witnesses will invite the nation of Israel to look by
faith to the Lamb of God, so they can wash their
robes and make them white in the blood of the
Lamb."

The two witnesses confronting the beast (Antichrist), Rev.11. (From
Luther's December Testament of 1522.)

THE PRODIGAL PLANET

JODI: *"I don't have to listen to you."*

JIMMY: *"No, you don't, but you might as well because you're going to stay here until I'm done. You can hear something for once, besides how pretty you are. Its obvious what you have been told all your life. You are pretty on the outside, but do you want to know what you are like on the inside? Jody! We can cover up our faces with makeup but we can't hide what's inside out hearts. I think our hearts are so wicked that this is what they look like to God."*

FILM CLIP #36 (See the Prophecy Survival Guide video)

Who rules from Jerusalem?

Dr. Kober:

"Actually, antichrist will first rule from Rome over a ten nation confederacy, which we call the revived Roman empire. According to Daniel 9:26, he comes out of Rome. But when his major enemy - under the kings of the north - has been removed, when Russia invades Israel and is destroyed, then he will move his military headquarters to Israel. According to the last verse of Daniel 11, He plants his tabernacles on the holy mountain. And this could only be Jerusalem. For 3 1/2 years he rules over Europe, and for the next 3 1/2 years, over the entire world."

Dr. Pentecost:

"When antichrist comes to exercise political authority, he will set up his headquarters between the seas in the glorious holy mountain. 'The glorious holy mountain' is a reference in the Old Testament (Daniel 11:45) to the city that God had chosen as the place where His Temple would be

And after threescore and two weeks shall Messiah be cut off, but not for himself: and the people of the prince that shall come shall destroy the city and the sanctuary; and the end thereof shall be with a flood, and unto the end of the war desolations are determined.

DAN 9:26

And he shall plant the tabernacles of his palace between the seas in the glorious holy mountain; yet he shall come to his end, and none shall help him.

DAN 11:45

92

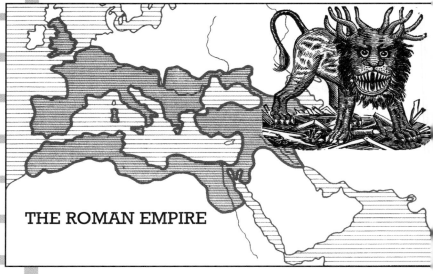

THE ROMAN EMPIRE

The revived Roman Empire under antichrist's rule is pictured in Daniel 7 as a terrifying beast.

THE ANTICHRIST

The Roman Prince of Daniel 7:27-28, as the counterfeit messiah.

built. Therefore, our conclusion is that the antichrist will rule the world as an imitation of the reign of Christ, from Jerusalem."

Dr. Price:

"Jerusalem is not only the center of antichrist's administration, but also the place of his religious authority. According to Daniel 9:27, antichrist makes a covenant with the Jewish people. This perhaps begins his religious hold on the city, because we know that the temple is rebuilt shortly after that - Revelation 11:1 - 2. And then in 2 Thessalonians 2:4 it says that the antichrist will seat himself in that temple, making himself out to be God. After that the judgments of God fall and disrupt his religious and political rule."

And he shall confirm the covenant with many for one week: and in the midst of the week he shall cause the sacrifice and the oblation to cease, and for the overspreading of abominations he shall make it desolate, even until the consummation, and that determined shall be poured upon the desolate.

DAN 9:27

At the mid-point of the tribulation, antichrist moves his headquarters from Rome to Jerusalem. (DAN 11:44-45)

THE PRODIGAL PLANET

JERRY: *"Stay with the unit. Don't get in there and get that drug out!"*

DAVID: *"Where's the other one?"*

JODI: *"Right behind us!"*

FILM CLIP #37 (See the Prophecy Survival Guide video)

PRODUCTION STILL

Russ Doughten sits on the guillotine during the filming of Image of the Beast.

What is the meaning of 1260?

Dr. Walvoord:

"It comes from the expression 'time, times, and half a time' - representing years: one year, plus 2 years, plus a half a year."

Dr. Kober:

"The number 1260 specifically is used several times in reference to the last part of the tribulation period. That second half is known as 'the great tribulation.' In Revelation 12:6 we read of these 1260 days. And then in verse 14 we read in reference to that period as it being time - one year, and times - two years, and 1/2 a time - a half a year. So the numbers are to be taken literally as a reference to the last half of the tribulation."

Dr. Pentecost:

"1260 days, according to the Jewish calendar, is three and a half years. According to the prophecy of Daniel's seventieth week, that week was to be divided into two equal parts, each having 1260 days. So the reference to those days in the book of Revelation is a reference to literal days. There would be a literal fulfillment of Daniel's prophecy of the seventy weeks."

And he shall speak great words against the most High, and shall wear out the saints of the most High, and think to change times and laws: and they shall be given into his hand until a time and times and the dividing of time.

But the judgment shall sit, and they shall take away his dominion, to consume it and to destroy it unto the end.

DAN 7:25-26

And the woman fled into the wilderness, where she hath a place prepared of God, that they should feed her there a thousand two hundred and threescore days.

REV 12:6

UNITE truck crashes through a house in Image of the Beast.

PRODUCTION NOTES

It was almost impossible to find someone who would let us crash a truck into his home, through the kitchen and out the back door. We believe that God provided the house and one of the world's greatest stunt men to drive the truck.

Don Thompson, Producer/Director

The Terminology and Chronology of the Tribulation

Daniel 9:27 "Covenant for one week... in the middle of the week cut off."

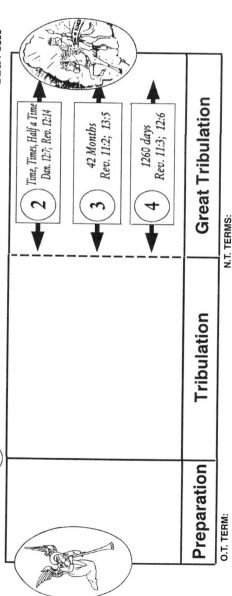

Second Advent

BEGINNING OF DANIEL'S 70TH WEEK

1

2 — *Time, Times, Half a Time* Dan. 12:7; Rev. 12:14

3 — *42 Months* Rev. 11:2; 13:5

4 — *1260 days* Rev. 11:3; 12:6

Preparation	Tribulation	Great Tribulation

O.T. TERM:

1. Time of Jacob's Trouble (Jer. 30:7)
2. Indignation (Isa. 20:20-21)
3. Trouble (Jer. 30:7; Dan. 12:1)

N.T. TERMS:

1. Great Tribulation (Rev. 2:22; 7:14)
2. Wrath (Rom. 5:9; 1Thess. 5:9)
3. Hour of Temptation (Rev. 3:10)

Manfred E. Kober, Th.D.

98

THE PRODIGAL PLANET

PEOPLE SINGING in a cave: *"Onward then ye people, join our happy throng. Blend with ours your voices, in the triumph song. Glory, laud and honor, unto Christ the King. This through countless ages, men and angels sing!"*

FILM CLIP #38 (See the Prophecy Survival Guide video)

PRODUCTION STILL

A serious moment in the film Image of the Beast.

What is Gog and Magog?

Dr. Price:

"The term Gog and Magog is found in Ezekiel 38 and 39, and also in Revelation 20. And there in Ezekiel, Gog is a title, like a ruler, whereas Magog is a people which Gog rules, and refers to an end-time ruler who will invade the nation of Israel with armies from the north."

Dr. Pentecost:

"In Ezekiel 38, that power to the north called Gog and Magog, that invades Israel, is said to come from the farthest north. Proceeding north from Jerusalem to the farthest north would bring you to the contemporary land of Russia. And many Bible teachers have felt that Russia will join with the Arab nations in an invasion of Israel during the tribulation period."

Dr. Kober:

"The term Gog and Magog is first used in Ezekiel 38 and 39. Gog is a ruler, Magog his people. The areas are Meshech and

Therefore thou son of man prophesy against Gog, and say, Thus saith the Lord God; behold, I am against thee, O Gog, the chief prince of Meshech and Tubal:

And I will turn thee back and leave but the sixth part of thee, and will cause thee to come up from the north parts, and will bring thee upon the mountains of Israel:

And I will smite thy bow out of thy left hand, and will cause thine arrows to fall out of thy right hand.

Thou shalt fall upon the mountains of Israel, thou, and all thy bands, and the people that is with thee: I will give thee unto the ravenous birds of every sort, and to the beasts of the field to be devoured.

EZ 39:1-4

The battle of Gog and Magog Prophesied and Preached

PRODUCTION NOTES

In the film Image of the Beast, we would need thousands of people and scenes of massive destruction. Don and Russ prayed about it. A few weeks later the Pope came to Des Moines and we filmed 600,000 people crowding to see him. Then later, Mt. St. Helen erupted and our crew filmed background footage of enormous destruction. So the scenes that they were concerned about were in the can even before the script was written.

Don Thompson, Producer/Director

Tubal. There's an army that will invade Israel in the middle of the tribulation period and will be totally destroyed by God in a supernatural way. Magog, Meshech, and Tubal were grandsons of Noah according to Genesis 10:2. And their descendants settled in what is present-day Russia."

EZEKIEL 39:17-19
And, thou son of man, thus saith the Lord God; Speak unto every feathered fowl, and to every beast of the field, Assemble yourselves, and come; gather yourselves on every side to my sacrifice that I do sacrifice for you, even a great sacrifice upon the mountains of Israel, that ye may eat flesh, and drink blood.
Ye shall eat the flesh of the mighty, and drink blood of the princes of the earth, of rams, of lambs, and of goats, of bullocks, all of them fatlings of Bashan.
And ye shall eat fat till ye be full, and drink blood till ye be drunken, of my sacrifice which I have sacrificed for you.

THE AFTERMATH OF THE BATTLE OF GOG AND MAGOG

A DISTANT THUNDER

The Seven Bowl Judgments of Revelation 16. (From Luther's Complete Bible, 1534.)

Is global warming related to the tribulation?

Dr. Kober:

"I'm not so sure there is a global warming. I read somewhere that the medium temperature on this planet has risen only one and a half degrees since the turn of the century. But the Bible does speak of the sudden and dramatic increase in heat on this planet. One of the judgments, in fact the fourth bowl judgment, will bring about the heating up of the sun and the scorching of mankind. If that is the case, the polar ice caps will be melting, raising the sea level by 200 feet, and probably destroying most of the world's large cities."

And the fourth angel poured out his vial upon the sun; and power was given unto him to scorch men with fire.

And men were scorched with great heat, and blasphemed the name of God, which hath power over these plagues: and they repented not to give him glory.

REV 16:8-9

Dr. Pentecost:

"Those judgments that involve heat in the tribulation period involve not so much the earth but the sun and the moon: catastrophes that are a divine judgment meted out

THE PRODIGAL PLANET

DAVID: *"We've been groaning and bellyaching about the heat. I think it's about to save our lives. God knows what He is doing, even if we don't!"*

FILM CLIP #39 (See the Prophecy Survival Guide video)

PRODUCTION STILL

The setting up of the guillotine in Image of the Beast.

on the earth. And it could be questioned that a gradual warming of the earth would be what is anticipated in those cataclysmic judgments in the convolution of the heavens during the tribulation period."

Dr. Price:

"People are terribly concerned today about environmental disasters created by man, but in the tribulation we'll see something far in excess of this, because God Himself will judge the earth with disasters far unparalleled by anything that has come before."

Behold, the day of the Lord cometh, cruel both with wrath and fierce anger, to lay the land desolate: and he shall destroy the sinners thereof out of it.

For the stars of heaven and the constellations thereof shall not give their light: the sun shall be darkened in his going forth, and the moon shall not cause her light to shine.

And I will punish the world for their evil, and the wicked for their iniquity; and I will cause the arrogancy of the proud to cease and will lay low the haughtiness of the terrible.

IS 13:9-11

The mourning of the kings of the earth, Revelation 18.
(Illustration from Luther's September Testament, 1522.)

THE PRODIGAL PLANET

NEWS ANNOUNCER: *"Already many nations are moving their troops over the Himalayan road built by West Pakistan and the Red Chinese to join forces with the technical might of its European allies. The only other obstacle in the troop movement from China to Palestine was the Euphrates River. And it appears now that the mighty river bed is dry, allowing free movement of troops and tanks toward Israel, the Galilee region near Haifa."*

FILM CLIP #40 (See the Prophecy Survival Guide video)

What is the role of the eastern armies?

Dr. Pentecost:

"The land of Israel will be invaded by the kings of the south - evidently Arab nations, by kings of the north - the Russian coalition, and then by the kings of the east. All that is said about them is that they come from east of the Euphrates River, so this could include an untold number from India, China, Japan, and the islands of the Pacific that are bent on preventing the return of Jesus Christ back to this earth."

Dr. Kober:

"The eastern armies are part of the campaign of Armageddon. They are mentioned in Daniel 11:44 as coming from the north and the east into Israel, whereupon the antichrist moves his headquarters from Rome, Italy, to Jerusalem, in Israel. According to Revelations 16:12, the Euphrates River dries up to allow for these kings of the east to enter Israel. And in Revelation 9:16 we read the awesome number of these demonized horsemen: two hundred million."

And the king shall do according to his will; and he shall exalt himself, and magnify himself above every god, and shall speak marvelous things against the God of gods, and shall prosper till the indignation be accomplished: for that is determined shall be done.

DAN 11:36

And the number of the army of the horsemen were two hundred thousand thousand: and I heard of them.

REV 9:16

But the tidings out of the east and out of the north shall trouble him: therefore he shall go forth with great fury to destroy, and utterly to make away many.

And he shall plant the tabernacles of his palace between the seas in the glorious holy mountain; yet he shall come to his end, and none shall help him.

DAN 11:44-45

THE PRODIGAL PLANET

DAVID: *"And he gathered them together to a place called in the Hebrew tongue Armageddon."*

FILM CLIP #41 (See the Prophecy Survival Guide video)

PRODUCTION NOTES

The film called for a major train and car crash. We discovered that Twentieth-Century Fox had a film with footage of a scene just like we needed. After much prayer we went to the Legal Department and found an attorney who was able to release the footage. We found a car that resembled the car in the accident and it all worked out fine.How do you get a neutron bomb to explode over Omaha, Nebraska? Now, that would be impossible. We filmed the Omaha skyline, but shot the actual scenes in Albuquerque, New Mexico. Eight blocks had to be empty, all lights, signs, water fountains had to be shut down. For five days the traffic was stopped for 30 seconds at a time as we shot the scenes, then everything resumed. It turned out to be the easiest part of the seven-week shoot.

Don Thompson, Producer/Director

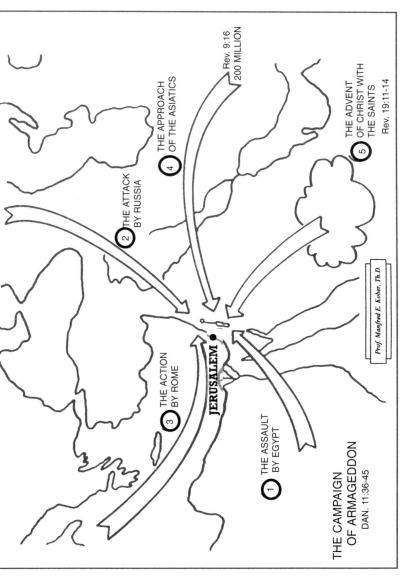

THE CAMPAIGN OF ARMAGEDDON
DAN. 11:36-45

1 THE ASSAULT BY EGYPT

2 THE ATTACK BY RUSSIA

3 THE ACTION BY ROME

4 THE APPROACH OF THE ASIATICS
Rev. 9:16
200 MILLION

5 THE ADVENT OF CHRIST WITH THE SAINTS
Rev. 19:11-14

JERUSALEM

Prof. Manfred E. Kober, Th.D.

THE CONVERGENCE OF THE WORLD'S ARMIES IN ISRAEL DURING THE CAMPAIGN OF ARMAGEDDON

What is the impact of these films?

Narrator:

"You know him as Reverend Turner. He is the executive producer of Mark IV Films. Russ Doughten, what was the purpose of making these films?"

Russ Doughten:

"Our purpose for making the films is to win people to the Lord. When I was a new Christian and read some of the prophecies, I didn't understand them very well, until I found a book that had them drawn out into charts and things that showed them interacting one with another. And I began to realize that prophecy made visual, like we can do it in a film, can be a very, very powerful way of helping people to first of all know about what is coming, and particularly that Christ is coming and it is important for them to relate to Him before He comes. Now, we work together to make the script, but the important part of it is that God's Spirit works through the script, the actors, the director, the editor, and on through the screen to the person that is watching, and they are drawn to Jesus Christ."

RUSSELL S. DOUGHTEN, JR.

Russ Doughten:

"The impact of these films has been marvelous. We believe that over 300 million people have seen 'A Thief in the Night', and this series. We also believe that after viewing the films, over 6

PRODUCTION STILL

million people have come to know Christ as their Savior. And the most marvelous thing is that each one who came, came by himself, one at a time. And perhaps now, Christ is reaching out to you and asking you to come to Him, right now, after this broadcast. Won't you come to Him?"

Russ Doughten in The Prodigal Planet.

THE PRODIGAL PLANET

DAVID: *"...To be part of God's kingdom or to have to live for an eternity with the agony and remorse and regret of those who reject Him and His love. Oh, Linda! God in His faithfulness has given you a choice!"*

FILM CLIP #42 (See the Prophecy Survival Guide video)

Will any part of the earth escape?

Dr. Walvoord:

"It says in Scripture that the great earthquake - the seventh bowl - is going to cover the whole earth, except for Israel. And it speaks of destroying the cities of nations, which is the word for gentiles. I take it that Israel escapes. This is confirmed by Zechariah 14 where there is house-to-house fighting in Israel on the very day of the Second Coming. And, of course, if you had Israel destroyed, there wouldn't be any house - to - house fighting."

Dr. Price:

"The Old Testament prophet Haggai said in the second chapter of his book, that God would shake all nations, and this refers to the Second Coming of Christ and the disasters that occur before that time. We also read in Zechariah 14, that there will be nations that will be left after that time, that will go up and worship the Lord in Jerusalem. So there will certainly be

Behold, the day of the Lord cometh, and thy spoil shall be divided in the midst of thee.

For I will gather all nations against Jerusalem to battle; and the city shall be taken, and the houses rifled, and the women ravished; and half the city shall go forth into captivity, and the residue of the people shall not be cut off from the city.

Then shall the Lord go forth, and fight against those nations, as when he fought in the day of battle.

ZECH 14:1-3

The 144,000 in heaven and the destruction of Babylon in Revelation 14. (Illustration from Luther's September Testament, 1522.)

PRODUCTION NOTES

Don had developed a scene involving a train hitting the war wagon. This would be almost impossible. When the idea was presented to the Santa Fe Railroad Company it met with hostility. Then Peg Courter, Assistant Director, had an idea, namely, that we offer the Railroad a copy of the footage to use in a safety film. That turned everything around. The railroad sent two men with two-way radios who slowed down and speeded up trains so the shoot could take place. We owned the Santa Fe Railroad for seven hours.

nations that will be left, but the devastation will be universal. And the point of this is seen in the fact that the sun is affected and that the stars in heaven will fall in the form of a meteor shower. That certainly is something that is not isolated."

For thus saith the Lord of hosts; Yet once, it is a little while, and I will shake the heavens, and the earth, and the sea, and the dry land;

And I will shake all nations, and the desire of all nations shall come: and I will fill this house with glory, saith the Lord of hosts.

HAG 2:6-7

In the sun, and moon, and stars,
Signs and wonders have appeared;
Earth has groaned with bloody wars,
And the hearts of men have feared.

Soon shall ocean's hoary deep,
Tossed with stronger tempest rise;
Darker storms the mountains sweep,
Fiercer lightnings rend the skies.

Dread alarms shall shake the proud,
Pale amazement, restless fear;
And amid the thunder-cloud
Shall the Judge of men appear.

But, though from his awful face,
Heaven shall fade, and earth shall fly,
Fear not ye, his chosen race,
Your redemption draweth nigh.

Reginald Heber

Prophecy Materials

Helpful materials available from Russ Doughten Films:
   1-800-247-3456

BOOK OF REVELATION CHART (seen on television)
   Large size: 19"x 33" -   Full color . . . .$11.95 + s&h
   Small size: 8"x 14"   -   Full color, 10 per pkg. . . . .$34.50 + s&h

PROPHECY VIDEOS (seen on television)
   A Thief in the Night - VHS, 69 minutes, color . . . . .$39.95 + s&h
   A Distant Thunder - VHS, 77 minutes, color . . . .$39.95 + s&h
   Image of the Beast - VHS, 93 minutes, color . . . . . .$39.95 + s&h
   The Prodigal Planet - VHS, 127 minutes, color . . . . .$39.95 + s&h

---

Publications by Manfred E. Kober, Th.D.
   An Illustrated Manual of the Tribulation . . . .$4.00 inc. s&h
   A Panorama of Prophecy -- End -Time Events
      Divinely Disclosed, 142 pages . . . .$29.95 inc. s&h
   Focus on the Future -- Exciting Expectations
      for Creation and Its Creatures, 172 pages . . . . .$29.95 inc. s&h
   All three above manuals are profusely illustrated with charts and
   maps. They are of great value to the layman and especially suited for
   pastors and Bible teachers.
   A set of over 120 graphics, charts and time lines on
   end times events, **some of which are used in this book.**
                     . . . .$20.00 + s&h
available from:
      Dr. Manfred Kober
      5907 Meredith Drive
      Des Moines, IA. 50322

Publications by J. Dwight Pentecost
   Prophecy for Today, Discovery House, 1989, 101 pages
   Things to Come, Zondervan, 1985, 633 pages

Publications by J. Randall Price
   Jerusalem in Prophecy, Harvest House, 1998, 434 pages
   Ready to Build, Harvest House, 1992, 288 pages
   Videos are available for both titles.

Publications by John F. Walvoord

Every Prophecy of the Bible, Chariot Victor, 1999, 688 pages
The Final Drama, Kregel, 1998, 192 pages
Major Bible Prophecies, Zondervan, 1996, 450 pages
Road to Armageddon, Nelson Word, 1999, 220 pages
End Times, Nelson Word, 1998, 243 pages

Publications by Charles C. Ryrie

Basic Theology, Victor Books, 1986, 544 pages
   Includes an excellent 100-page section on prophecy.
Come Quickly Lord Jesus, Harvest House, 1996, 142 pages
   *Superb book on the rapture. Out of print, but a few copies
   may be found at Faith Baptist Bible College Bookstore.*

General books on prophecy

Understanding End Times Prophecy, Paul Benware
   Moody, 1995, 309 pages
World News and Bible Prophecy, Charles Dyer
   Tyndale, 1993, 303 pages
Three Worlds in Conflict, The High Drama of Prophecy,
   Stanley A. Ellisen, Multnomah, 1998, 224 pages
Are These the Last Days?, R. G. Gromacki
   Regular Baptist Press, 1970, 149 pages
The Bible and Future Events, Leon J. Wood
   Zondervan, 1983, 373 pages
The End Times, Herman Hoyt
   Brethren Missionary Herald, 256 pages
Exploring the Future, John Phillips
   Loizeaux Brothers, 1992, 413 pages

**You can order any of the above books or videos by phone, e-mail, or fax
from:**

Faith Baptist Bible College Bookstore
1900 NW 4th Street
Ankeny, IA 50021
Phone: 515-964-7946
Fax: 515-964-4895
E-mail: fbbcbooks@aol.com

Visit Russ Doughten Films on the Internet at
www.rdfilms.com

Movies that touch the heart with the good news of Jesus Christ.

A DRAMATIC SERIES OF THE END-TIMES

ENGLISH AND SPANISH

1-800-247-3456

Russ Doughten Films

WWW.rdfilms.com

PROPHECY 4-PACK
- Classic End-Times series
- Award-winning acting & special effects
- Free 14"x 7^7/8" End-Times Chart in pack
- Available in Spanish

$114.95!

End-Times Prophecy Chart
- Featured in *Image of The Beast* and *The Prodigal Planet.*
- Available in two sizes:
  33"x 18^1/2" UV coated, **$11.95**
  14"x 7^7/8" 10-pack only, **$34.50**

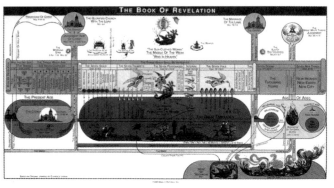

HEALING PACK
Nite Song
The Healing
The Paradise Trail
Movies that touch
the searching
heart.

$59.95

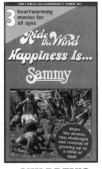

CHILDREN'S VIDEO SET
Sammy
Happiness Is...
Ride The Wind
Inspirational and
exciting family fun

$44.95

THE PACKS
ARE A GREAT
VALUE

ACTION PACK
The Shepherd
Heaven's Heroes
Blood On The Mountain
Inspirational
dramas at their best

$59.95

Free catalog listing of
all 24 films available,
call:
1-800-247-3456
WWW.RDFILMS.COM

POWER PACK
Coach
Test Of Faith
Brother Enemy
Rock.. It's Your Decision
Powerful
challenges for
today's youth

$69.95

FAMILY PACK
Survival
Home Safe
All The King's Horses
A celebration
of family values

$59.95

Share Your Faith
S E M I N A R

A comprehensive discipleship training program. Easy-to-follow instructions. Emphasizes the use of movie videos as an effective witnessing tool. Based on successful live Share Your Faith seminars. Suitable for groups or individuals. Developed by Mustard Seed International

INCLUDES: Instruction Manual, 120-page Workbook, 2-tape Video of a Live Seminar (194 minutes), Bible Study, Six Steps to Successful Film Evangelism Booklet, 2 New Testaments, Ready Reference Guides

PLUS: 1 Feature-length Movie Video.

THE SHARE YOUR FAITH SEMINAR IS valued

At $225.00. You pay **$189.95**

Russ Doughten Films, Inc.
1-800-247-3456